DREAM OF A RED FACTORY

DREAM OF
A RED FACTORY

The Legacy of High Stalinism
in China

Deborah A. Kaple

New York   Oxford
Oxford University Press
1994

Oxford University Press

Oxford   New York   Toronto
Delhi   Bombay   Calcutta   Madras   Karachi
Kuala Lumpur   Singapore   Hong Kong   Tokyo
Nairobi   Dar es Salaam   Cape Town
Melbourne   Auckland   Madrid

and associated companies in
Berlin   Ibadan

Published by Oxford University Press, Inc.,
200 Madison Avenue, New York, New York 10016

Library of Congress Cataloging-in-Publication Data
Kaple, Deborah A.
Dream of a red factory : the legacy of high Stalinism
in China / Deborah A. Kaple.
p. cm.   Includes bibliographical references and index.
ISBN 0-19-508315-6
1. Industrial organization—China.
2. Industrial management—China.
3. Industrial organization—Soviet Union.
4. Industrial management—Soviet Union.
5. Socialism—China.
6. Socialism—Soviet Union. I. Title.
HD70.C5K37   1994
658'.00951'09045—dc20   92-45579

1 3 5 7 9 8 6 4 2

Printed in the United States of America
on acid-free paper

To my best friend and husband,
Miguel Angel Centeno

Preface

Dream of a Red Factory: The Legacy of High Stalinism in China is a study of enduring communist power and authority, and like China's most beloved novel, *Dream of a Red Chamber*, its method is to capture the essence of a larger society through the prism of a smaller world, in this case, through the eyes of factory managers and workers. It is the story of the Chinese Communist Party's (CCP) "dream" of transforming China into a modern, socialist, industrialized country and, in particular, the way in which the Party went about changing the structure of factory administration. This book is also a reinterpretation of the Sino-Soviet relationship, about which so much has been written and, until now, about which so little has been known. Finally, in examining the role of imported ideas in the process of social change, this book chronicles the CCP's reliance on an idealized version of the Soviet "model" and how Stalinism ultimately became an integral part of Chinese communism.

In 1949 when the communists came to power, they had some specific goals for China, like socialist industrialization, but few concrete plans. This book demonstrates how they expanded their goals to include not only socialist industrialization but worker socialization and control as well, for China's population was large, uneducated, and not necessarily pro-communist. Effecting socialist industrialization in China would mean more than changing managers at a few factories; it would mean that workers had to be trained and reeducated as "socialists" and that managers had to learn Marxism-Leninism in order to control and mobilize the workers correctly. With this huge task facing them, the Chinese Communist Party instinctively turned to the Soviet Union for help.

The USSR, however, did not provide the answers, for the relationship between Stalin and Mao was never good, and the USSR was badly strapped for cash after its disastrous war experience. Undeterred and with few other choices, the CCP launched a huge translation program from Russian to Chinese so that China could immediately begin its planned industrialization based on the Soviet experience. This turn of events, though unnoticed by the outside world, shaped the style and form of communism that eventually developed in China. These neglected original sources that the Chinese translated from Russian form the basis of this book.

What did the CCP choose to translate into Chinese, and why? What was the "Soviet model" that they soon urged on the Chinese people? This book looks at the primary sources (the Chinese translations and the original Russian books) in order to understand not only the CCP vision and intention in this transition but also what the Chinese communists imported and how this affected China's development.

One of the important findings of this book is that the CCP based its work in industrial management on the Soviet Fourth Five-Year Plan of 1946–1950. Because the CCP's emulation of this particular period so affected later Chinese developments and because this period of Soviet history has been overlooked by Western specialists, Chapter 2 examines industrial management and organization in the USSR during these years. The CCP did not import some generic "Soviet model" but emulated the methods and techniques of Stalinism, in particular, a model that existed during the bleak and oppressive postwar recovery period known as "High Stalinism." Through Chapter 2's examination of Soviet management and organizational techniques during this period, the elements of High Stalinism emerge. These were the Communist Party's primacy in factory management, the formation of "mass" organizations in all factories and enterprises, the militarization of management rhetoric, the creation of "reeducation" classes for workers and managers, and the equation of patriotism with plan fulfillment. Along with the various management techniques and methods that the CCP imported from Stalin's USSR came all of the High Stalinist elements, which later appeared as an important aspect of Chinese industrial life.

The Soviet management model as it actually existed between 1946 and 1950 focused on worker training programs, recruitment methods, and various mobilization techniques. One of the principal methods touted in the Soviet press, and subsequently by the CCP, was the use of mass campaigns to push workers to produce. An examination of the historical record, however, reveals one major fact that had lasting consequences for China's development and that the Chinese could not have gleaned from their reading of the press and journal articles. The campaign method was so disruptive to the normal rhythm of production that the Fourth Five-Year Plan was secretly dropped in 1947.

The problems of this Soviet "model" did not appear in the CCP's introduction to the Chinese people between 1949 and 1953, as Chapter 2 shows. Instead, the Party focused on convincing the population that the Soviets had created the best socialist industrial management model possible. It was an enticing argument because of the apparent parallels between the Soviet conditions of 1946–1950 and the Chinese circumstances of 1949–1953. For instance, in 1946, the Soviets were recovering from a war and were faced with training a new work force to begin the recovery effort; the Chinese were also recovering from long-term strife and also faced the task of creating an industrial proletariat from a mostly rural population. The CCP praised Soviet methods and techniques from this period as the way to solve these problems. The Chinese translated and disseminated the USSR's Seven Precepts of Management, which mainly ensured Communist Party control over management, and the Soviet technique of using "mass" methods in the factory by relying on the Party, the labor union, and the youth group, all of which were to organize, control, and train workers.

Chapter 3 introduces the Soviet model of enterprise management as the Chinese saw it, based on Chinese translations of Soviet materials, books, articles, and journals. The model's optimistic tone reflects the CCP's lack of experience and acquaintance with the workings of Soviet socialism. The clear lesson in this literature is, again, the strength and power of the Soviet Communist Party in every aspect of production and management of enterprises.

Chapters 4, 5, and 6 look at the CCP's three goals that would realize its "dream of a red factory" in the period between 1949 and 1953, illustrating how the most important High Stalinist precept of Party control became the outstanding characteristic of the Chinese industrial management strategy. Chapter 4 concentrates on the goal of industrialization and how the CCP approached the task of managing a socialist factory. The Chinese communists took a two-pronged approach: They, like the Soviets, issued a formal statement called the Industrial Management Mechanism, and they created an indigenous program called Democratization of Management that functioned in the factories as well. Both of these management mechanisms operating simultaneously caused confusion but also strengthened the power of the Party in factory management. In the formal management mechanism, the CCP copied the original Soviet precepts and also increased the number of those emphasizing party control. In the Democratization movement, the Party controlled all the committees and groups that were formed.

Chapter 5 turns to the important issue of worker socialization, for without a strong education and reeducation program, the Communist Party could not solidify its control over the population and could not pursue its "dream" of socialist factories. It had to create a working class in China. Again, the CCP took a two-tiered approach: It subjected the workers to an education program that taught them the new socialist "worldview," and it made organizational changes in the management hierarchy of factories. The CCP's new worldview, which was written as workers' handbooks and distributed at work, was a complete reinterpretation of Chinese history as the history of class exploitation, including a new section about the significant role of the Communist Party. Here the CCP introduced the concepts of "class war," "class struggle," and "thought control," all of which were used to great effect for many years. To supplement the teachings, the CCP then established Soviet-style factory "mass" organizations, including factory Party committees, labor unions, and youth groups.

This large-scale reliance on "mass" organizations in the factory was the CCP's main vehicle for effecting political control of the population, as seen in Chapter 6. Through these organizations, the Communist Party was able to mobilize, teach, and control the movement of all members by channeling them into mass campaigns. The CCP saw such campaigns as the best way to achieve large economic goals and also to manipulate and control the workers. The CCP's campaigns soon exhibited the influence of its reliance on the harsh High Stalinist sources. The CCP's first campaigns were organized to achieve economic goals, but these were followed by campaigns with more blatantly political goals. Soon the political goals were more prominent than the economic aims, and with each campaign came more fear and intimidation as the CCP, like the Soviet Party, coerced its workers into fulfilling its goals.

This book illustrates how from the beginning the early structures and lessons that the CCP took from the written High Stalinist sources created a powerful and authoritative Communist Party in China. After this book was completed, I spent several months in the newly opened Soviet Communist Party archives in Moscow. This new research on the Sino-Soviet relationship of the 1950s confirms the conclusions that this book reaches, both about the relationship and the consequences of China's mass study program of the Soviet model in the early 1950s.

The ideas borrowed from High Stalinism combined with the CCP goal of political control had several consequences for China, some of which endure even today. First, the environment at the factories and in society in general became politicized more quickly than otherwise would have been possible. Second, the CCP had more power than its Soviet counterpart did, in both industry and society, and third, the Party's intrusion and coercion in management was great very early on. Fourth, deep and divisive class lines in society were drawn, with clear ramifications for the bitter "class struggle" that indeed developed later. Both the CCP's reliance on an idealized description of a bleak stage of Soviet history and its own drive for political control in society helped develop the Communist Party's legacy of coercion and authoritarian power, which endures even today.

Moscow   D.A.K.
January 1993

Acknowledgments

My good fortune as I worked on this book is evident in the long list of institutions that provided assistance. I gratefully acknowledge the support of the Harriman Institute at Columbia University; the East Asia National Resource Center at Stanford University; the Center for International Studies, the Council on Regional Studies, and the sociology department at Princeton University; the Mellon Foundation; the Social Science Research Council; and the International Research and Exchanges Board. In the former USSR, I extend my thanks to the USSR Academy of Sciences' Institute of the Far East, Institute of Scientific Information, and Institute of World Economy and International Relations. In the People's Republic of China, I thank the Chinese Academy of Social Sciences' Institute on the Soviet Union and Eastern Europe.

I also have been blessed with a long list of supporters and friends, all of whom contributed in some way to this book (and none of whom is responsible for any of its errors). At Princeton University, I thank the Sociology Department and the East Asian Studies Department; my original dissertation committee of Gil Rozman, Lynn White, and Frank Dobbin; and my mentors and professors, Mel Tumin and Marvin Bressler. At the Harriman Institute, I thank my fellow postdoctoral scholars Gerald Easter, Roger Peterson, and Ned Walker and especially my friend and adviser, Kevin Laney. I also must mention the many colleagues and friends in Beijing and Moscow who helped me, in particular my good friend Ida Aronovna Kats.

Joseph Berliner deserves special mention as an unswerving supporter of me and my work and as one who read the manuscript several times and provided insightful comments, and I thank also the anonymous readers for Oxford University Press who did a great job of reviewing the manuscript. My thanks to Oxford University Press's Nancy Lane and Edward Harcourt, whose professionalism and talent have made this process a pleasure. I also owe a great debt to John S. Major, my dear friend and colleague who somehow stayed interested until the end, as well as to James R. Millar; Jeff, Edie, and Walter Blattner; Bob, Edie, and David Engel; Sally Paxton, Annie Reynolds, and of course my close friends, the Swegle family.

My most heartfelt thanks goes to my family, who always stands behind me no matter what I do. I feel lucky to be part of this wonderful Ohio family, which includes Jack, Pat, and Addie Kaple; Travis Horstman; Esther Kaple; Kim and Rick Stuck and their family; Dawn and David Roebuck and their family; and Julia and Bob Hare and their family. Most of all, I thank my husband Miguel Angel Centeno for sharing his knowledge and enthusiasm in making this book as good as it is.

Contents

List of Tables

Note on Transliteration

There is no easy way to solve the problem of correctly rendering Russian or Chinese words into English. In this text, I have tried to be consistent throughout, so that a reader who knows either language will not be confused. I have allowed convention to prevail in several cases, where a word has already become familiar spelled in a certain way. Hence, the text includes words like Gorky (instead of Gorkii), or Dalny (instead of Dal'nii), or Chiang Kai-shek.

DREAM OF A RED FACTORY

A stand can be made against an invasion by an army; no stand can be made against invasion by an idea.

Victor Hugo

1

Modern China's Stalinist Roots

In the late 1980s, the world watched as the two leading communist regimes grappled with serious challenges to their authority and power. In China, the Chinese Communist Party (the CCP) remained firmly in charge by ordering tanks to crush its vocal opposition. In the USSR, the Soviet Communist Party tried to use tanks and failed. The collapse of the hard-liner coup in August 1991 signaled the end of over seventy years of the Communist Party of the Soviet Union (the CPSU) and its domination over Soviet society.

Both a return to such authoritarian practices in China and the total disintegration of the CPSU would have been unimaginable just a few years ago. These dramatic changes have led many observers to reflect on the reasons behind the failure of Soviet communism, but given the actual social, political, and economic deterioration that we now know characterized communism in the former USSR and Eastern Europe, the more interesting question is how the hard-liners have retained power so successfully in China. The latter is the starting point of this study, which explores the roots of Communist Party control in China.

The origins of Chinese communist power and authority are, ironically, rooted in Soviet communism.[1] The years of bitter defeats and Guomindang Party betrayals, the time spent in Yenan,[2] and the long years of the war against Japan also influenced the development of Chinese communism. The Yenan years were particularly important to shaping Mao Zedong's political beliefs and strengthening communist resolve. In 1949, he reflected this resolve and his deeply felt nationalism when he proclaimed that China "will no longer be a nation subject to insult and humiliation." "We have stood up!" he asserted.[3]

That same year, the very real prospect of taking over a country of 600 million people demanded much more. In one of history's many ironies, less than two months after the Chinese Communist Party took power, Chairman Mao and his entourage were on a train to Moscow, en route to what would be another unequal relationship with another imperialistic power, Stalin's USSR.

Mao stayed in Moscow from early December 1949 until mid-February 1950. On February 14, the Soviets and Chinese announced their new agreement, the Treaty of Friendship, Alliance, and Mutual Assistance Between the Union of Soviet Socialist Republics and the People's Republic of China.[4] The Soviets often have been criticized for the meager assistance to China that the agreement stipulated, and for the most part, the pact mainly addresses joint Chinese–Soviet actions in the face of renewed Japanese aggression. Such criticism, however, misses the real significance of the Sino-Soviet accord: Mao came back to China with the legitimacy of having been recognized by the world's greatest communist regime, and he brought with him a plan of action. Not only could he now claim to have Soviet endorsement, which lent him and his Communist Party an enormous amount of prestige, but he also had in hand a model for China's development into an industrialized socialist power.

The model that Mao and the CCP had in mind for China has been and remains critical to understanding the CCP's power and authority. Many of the patterns and structures of political power that were adopted and adapted during the 1949–1953 period prevail today. Even so, few Western scholars have critically evaluated the early years of the People's Republic of China's (PRC) development.[5] Until now, scholarly work on the 1950s has focused on more dramatic events, such as the land reform program, the Hundred Flowers Campaign, or the Sino-Soviet split. Such analyses generally gloss over or overlook the crucial first years of China's transformation and the process of studying and emulating the Soviet model.

To understand the origins of the Chinese Communist Party's power and, in turn, the events in Tiananmen in 1989, we must look again at the model of 1949–1953. What was it, and indeed, what was the "Soviet model?" The Western literature on China presents a confusing picture of the 1949-1953 model, because scholars have neglected to take a close look at the actual Soviet model that the Chinese studied and have failed to define it properly.[6] If there had been a clearer understanding about the origins of the Chinese model in the early years, for instance, we would immediately have seen that Mao's conception of bureaucracy, which later emerged in his criticism of the Soviet management system, was little more than the Stalinist system about which he had read in the early 1950s.[7] The Cultural Revolution charges of Soviet "revisionism," which included an alleged loosening of Party vigilance over worker behavior, and a de-emphasis of nonmaterial incentives during the late Stalin years, reflected little more than Mao's use of the Soviet model to fight domestic political battles, for as I shall show, nothing could be further from the truth of the postwar USSR.[8]

Again, instead of challenging this CCP picture of the Soviet management model, we have spent time defining Maoism as a system that was completely different from the Stalinist one on which it was based.[9] Andrew Walder comes closest to the truth in a 1982 article in which he concludes that Maoism is a primeval offshoot of Stalinism.[10] But his definition of Maoism—the eradication of incentives, the cult of leadership, the destruction of administrative staffs that checked the power of line management, and the increasing pressures to conform not only in action but also in thought—almost perfectly matches the Soviet "model" as it existed under the late Stalin.[11] In other words, we cannot view the Chinese administrative system as a genuine departure from Stalinist methods, but instead, we must view it as a close copy of a particular type of Stalinism.[12]

This book explores the Communist Party's power by looking closely at the PRC's industrial management model as it developed between 1949 and 1953 and, in a bit of sleuthing, by examining the original Soviet texts that appeared in Chinese during that period. This points us in the direction of the origins of the early Chinese model of industrial management and what the CCP hoped to create in the early 1950s. That is the focus of the next section.

Reading the Soviet Press of 1946–1950

One of the most striking findings of this study is that the Chinese communists consciously studied and attempted to adopt Stalin's recovery model of the immediate postwar period, 1946 to 1950. This is clearly the case in industrial management, for nearly all of the Chinese articles and journals that detailed changes and innovations between 1949 and 1953 cited examples from the so-called Stalin Fourth Five-Year Plan. In addition, the CCP's interest in the USSR of the mid- to late 1940s is reflected in its choice of books to translate into Chinese, as found in the equivalent of *Books in Print*, which is called the *Chinese General Title Catalogue*[13] for the years 1949 to 1953. China's interest in the Soviet experience is immediately obvious, for in the span of a few years, the CCP translated and printed in Chinese thousands of Soviet books, including volumes on the USSR's economy, political system, social structure, industry, and Party history. It is also apparent from the translations that the CCP wanted to look in detail at the USSR's "victorious" Fourth Five-Year Plan period of 1946 to 1950.

Why did the CCP expend such energy to translate all of these books? China had urgent needs, and the CCP wanted to begin immediately on its proclaimed goals of industrialization and the creation of an urban proletariat. Direct Soviet assistance was minimal in the 1949–1953 period, as I shall elaborate. As a consequence, the Chinese communists read and translated the Soviet books in order to import the necessary ideas, methods, and practical knowledge about Soviet socialism. As I shall discuss at length later in this chapter, Soviet books and articles were a major source of information about the model in the 1949–1953 period.

The CCP's quest for its "dream of a red factory," for ideas about embarking on socialist industrialization, is the focus of this book. The Chinese communists looked for manuals on how to organize socialist industry, train workers, motivate them to produce well, and ensure that the people did as the Communist Party mandated. The "Industrial Management" section of the *Chinese General Title Catalogue* reflects the CCP's interests in its listing of translated Soviet books that discuss socialist management, employee relations, the role of the manager, and worker motivation.[14]

With these sources, along with the myriad Chinese journal and newspaper articles from the 1949–1953 period, it is possible to reconstruct the CCP's interpretation of the Soviet model. This assumes, of course, that the books, articles, and monographs that were published in various parts of China after 1949 were at least sanctioned by the Chinese Communist Party. There is no way to know who read them, or even to whom they were addressed, but certainly the extensive discussions of many of the translated books and articles in the Chinese national industrial management literature in the early 1950s implied the Party's approval.[15]

What is the significance of the CCP's having translated and read this Soviet postwar literature on industrial organization and management? As I shall argue at length later in this book, this was a harsh stage of Soviet history known as "High Stalinism," a period that has also been called the "return of the revolution from above."[16] It was a time when the Soviet Communist Party was completely in control of all spheres of production, as well as all aspects of life outside the factory. The most important consequence of translating this literature into Chinese was that the CCP was able to learn and use the High Stalinist lessons of total Party control, and it was able on this basis to justify its own complete usurpation of power, in both the factory and society.

Total Party control was the message in the CCP's earliest translations of articles about management. For instance, in 1950, the Chinese communists prepared and issued handbooks of translations from the Soviet and East European press about the Soviet experience. Volume 3 of the collection called *Xuexi sulian qiye gongzuo jinyan* (We study the experience of Soviet enterprise work) is called "Problems of the Party–Masses Relationship in the Enterprise," but it is nothing more than a compilation of translated articles from the Soviet and East European press about Party work in factories.[17] The main point of each article is that strong Party control in the enterprise was absolutely essential to the plan's fulfillment.

Supreme party control and authority in industry and, indeed, in all aspects of life was the essence of High Stalinism.

The Influence of High Stalinism

High Stalinism[18] was the most salient feature of the Fourth Five-Year Plan period and Soviet postwar life, so it is no accident that the Chinese communists would encounter it in their reading of the Soviet literature and in their search for a model to guide China's transformation. One of the CCP's major goals in 1949 was to turn China into a modern, industrialized, socialist country. This meant, naturally, that the CCP sought ideas and materials on management and organization, for which it relied on the USSR's postwar experience. When the CCP translated and imported from the postwar sources the Soviet "blueprint" for socialized industry, it brought into China the practices of High Stalinism.

High Stalinism in postwar Soviet society meant the total supremacy of Stalin in all matters. He had triumphed over all internal enemies, as evidenced by the massive purges of the 1930s and early 1940s, and then had emerged victorious in World War II in the Soviet defeat of the Germans. Now Stalin could add international acclaim to his domestic adulation. In the words of one Russian historian, "The victory turned him finally into a god."[19] After the war, he was the indisputable expert on all matters, from linguistics to science policy. His influence was seen in administration as well.

In industrial management, High Stalinism had basically five aspects: Party control over management, the use of "mass methods," the widespread militarization of management, worker education and reeducation, and the equation of patriotism with plan fulfillment. In this management system, politics were more important than economics, and the Communist Party representatives were more influential and powerful than the nonParty managers. The goals were economic growth and the attainment of plan targets at any cost.

The first and most salient feature of High Stalinism was Communist Party control over all economic decisions at every level. During World War II, the Communist Party of the Soviet Union relied on very intrusive methods of control in factories to push the workers to produce. At each turn, the industrial management literature stressed how useful both small and mass meetings were. The Party organization and the labor union called the workers together for mandatory daily, weekly, and monthly meetings, and this practice continued in the postwar period.[20]

A second feature of this model was the use of "mass" methods, such as production campaigns, which were explained in great detail in all of the Soviet management handbooks. Mass campaigns were used to encourage the workers to achieve various goals, like the attainment of higher productivity or the reduction of waste. Such campaigns would seem to be perfectly suited to a country that was cash poor but rich in human resources. With massive supervision, great goals could be accomplished with little money.

The third feature, which at least in part was a manifestation of the militarization that Soviet society underwent during World War II, was the pervasive use of military terms in the management literature.[21] "Agitators" (those who propagandized for the Party in the enterprise) were referred to as the Communist Party's "arsenal"; their information was called "fighting facts and figures," and they regularly issued "fighting reports" (*boevie*). Agitators were also the "vanguard" who propagandized with the "banners of Bolshevik words." Wall newspapers were referred to as "battle weapons," and the quick reports were known as "lightening appeals" and "fighting leaflets." Knowledge of the factory's reserves was also called the Party's "strongest weapon." Propagandists were told that the workers must be taught to see their participation in socialist competitions as a "blood deal," that is, as very close to their hearts.[22]

The fourth feature of the Soviet model of this period was Stalin's belief that people could be educated and changed. This was manifest in the innumerable Party programs aimed at making the workers conversant with Marxism-Leninism, at "shaping" their attitude toward work, and at "improving" their political consciousness. This meant constant training and close supervision of workers at their jobs by the enterprise Party cell and labor union. During this period, the Party continuously directed an enormous amount of propaganda toward Soviet workers. (It would appear that either the Party assumed that the masses were unable to absorb the lessons of Marxism-Leninism and translate them into their work habits or that the workers resisted the barrage of propaganda.)

The last feature of the Soviet model of 1946–1950 was the linking of economic goals with patriotism. The agitators made it clear that each worker's job, no matter how small a contribution it might be, was vital to the economic recovery and the development of socialism. Even menial tasks in the enterprise were linked with national economic goals.

Each of these five characteristics permitted and supported the active intervention and supervision by the CPSU at every level of economic organization. The Soviet management model of 1946–1950, in short, was an exercise in the political power and authority of the Communist Party. As an economic model, however, it was deeply flawed and unworkable in practice. As we shall see in Chapter 2, the Soviets, in fact, quietly abandoned the Fourth Five-Year Plan and relied on the methods that did work, the management techniques of coercion and force.

In contrast with the glittering propaganda that the Chinese read, the Soviet population lived with great privation and hardship during the postwar period. As war victors, they had hoped to live lives free of terror, shortages, and campaigns, but the war had convinced Stalin of socialism's invincibility, and he saw no reason to rest. On February 9, 1946, in a speech at the Bolshoi Theater, Stalin made clear his intention to use unrelenting pressure to continue the process of socialist industrialization, even in the face of mass war-weariness. The Soviet postwar literature that the Chinese read emphasized that such a recovery could not have taken place without the strong leadership of the Communist Party.

Today as we examine this strong Party leadership, there appears to be a very fine line between Party strength and Party coercion. Either the CCP saw the Soviet system for what it was and ignored it, or it simply did not see the system as coercive. Some believe that Mao Zedong saw how important and powerful Stalin was and wanted to emulate Stalin in China.[23] This would imply that Mao understood the nature of Soviet socialism and decided to adopt it nonetheless. Although this question cannot be answered directly, it can be approached by outlining the CCP's perception of the Soviet model.[24]

China's View of the Soviet Model

The Chinese communists were impressed by the Soviet recovery from the devastation of a major world war.[25] They often noted that the Soviets had suffered more war damage than had any other country and yet had recovered more quickly than the others.[26] The CCP's view of the USSR after the war, as reflected in post-1949 Chinese publications, was that Soviet workers toiled selflessly, without wasting time or materials, to reconstruct their "wonderful life-style."[27] The Chinese communists wrote that the Soviet Union's postwar recovery was proof of the superiority of socialism over capitalism. This same strength was to be used in helping the international working class liberate itself, as in the Soviets helping the Chinese.[28]

The CCP was also impressed with the orderliness and organization of Soviet society and the workplace. Chinese observers called it an ideal society, a utopia, even a "socialist paradise" (*shehui zhuyide leyuan*).[29] The Chinese wrote that the rapid Soviet recovery was natural because it was a society founded by workers and for workers, and therefore, progress was inevitable. It was said that Soviet workers were so thankful that they had nothing but warm feelings toward their country and their work.[30] The Chinese communists seemed convinced that such gains for and by the workers could be realized only under socialism.[31]

The CCP attributed these achievements to strong Communist Party leadership.[32] The Chinese emphasized that with such leadership, the Soviets had organized society to the benefit of the workers; they had established a planned economy that eliminated all contradictions and allowed the workers to flourish; and they had structured the workplace to facilitate campaigns and emulation programs that guaranteed high productivity. One Chinese observer of a Soviet factory noted approvingly that the plant was so well organized that "it is difficult for the workers to lag behind."[33]

Once the decision was made for the top leadership to go to Moscow in December 1949, the CCP began a full-fledged propaganda campaign that introduced the Soviet model to the Chinese people. The CCP was eager to present the best of the Soviet system to China's citizens. A Chinese delegate to the Soviet May Day celebration in 1950 returned from Moscow and reported in a radio broadcast that the Soviet state took good care of its workers. She discussed the "happy life led by Soviet women and children," especially those who worked in factories. Childbirth is an honor in the USSR, she said, and therefore "every factory has its own nursery with specially trained nurses." In addition, she noted that the factories donated large sums of money to establish children's palaces, which supplemented the education at school.[34] One Chinese author of a text about the working class emphasized that the Soviet Union was a perfect society, a society of the type that China would try to create.[35]

The Chinese also paid close attention to the way in which the Soviets appeared to succeed in plan fulfillment, especially the Soviet use of campaigns, slogans, and worker competitions. Soon, the Chinese had adopted and adapted various Soviet methods, such as the Stakhanovite program to increase labor productivity. Not long after communist "liberation," Chinese journals and newspapers began to emulate the Soviet programs, even down to the details. Slogans such as "We Salute the Model Workers!" began to appear in Chinese journals in the early 1950s. These typically featured a small picture of the workers alongside a short blurb that explained their achievements in production competitions in various Chinese factories. For instance, one worker was said to have completed his one-year plan quota in five months, and another was quoted as saying that his heroic labor achievements would not have been possible without the leadership of the Communist Party.[36]

One of the reasons for Soviet successes, as the CCP presented it, was the Soviet method of workplace organization, which relied on the work of the Party, the labor union, and the youth groups. *Gongren ribao* (Workers' daily) reporter Zhou Ming was one of the first to file reports from the Soviet Union about how factories were organized.[37] For instance, he reported on the factory committees, the workshop committees, and the successful use of small groups (*xiao zu*) of the labor union. Writing about the labor union's role during a socialist competition at a Moscow knitting factory, he noted that every labor union representative had his own plan and that every day, on his own, he checked on the workers' progress. Every ten days the small group's plan was verified, and then the group reported to the workshop and factory committee. In the event that the "ten-day plan" was not fulfilled, there had to be a good explanation. To the CCP, this seemed very orderly and quite successful.

From its reading of the Soviet press, then, the CCP's perception of the model was favorable. Stalin's prestige was at its peak, and the Soviet Union had recovered rapidly from the devastation of war, had restored industry, and even had surpassed its prewar levels. As far as the Chinese could discern from their reading, the key to this success was the Communist Party control and organization at every level. But a few questions still remain: Why did the CCP choose the period of High Stalinism, and why did it then rely so heavily on written materials, instead of Soviet expert advice and assistance?

Why High Stalinism?

For all of the emphasis that the Chinese (and this book) placed on the original Soviet sources, the reader should not be led to believe either that these materials accurately reflected the situation that existed in the postwar USSR or that the Chinese communists understood and interpreted them correctly. The Soviet books and articles that the Chinese read and translated were, for the most part, propaganda pieces. As such, they presented a very appealing picture of the Soviet Fourth Five-Year Plan. No doubt, it was attractive as a total model of economic development. Not only could the CCP claim that the model represented Marxism-Leninism in practice; it also appeared to present the plans for a genuine economic recovery.

Again, it must be said that we have little indication of how much the CCP and Mao himself understood the Stalinist socialist model. That is, how much of the Chinese coverage of the Soviet Union in the early 1950s was simply propaganda, and how much of it did the Chinese communists actually believe?

The Chinese decision to turn to the High Stalinist literature in early 1950 was probably shaped by several important facts: the poor relationship between Stalin and Mao, the meager assistance from the Soviets in the early 1950s, and the CCP's consequent reliance on written materials instead of hands-on experience with the workings of the Soviets' postwar model.

In the first instance, China's adoption of the Soviet model between 1949 and 1953 was hampered by the cool relationship between Stalin and Mao. There had long been a rift between the two, which probably can be attributed to both competition and a hint of racism.[38] Stalin made it clear that he did not trust the Chinese leader,[39] and he also knew that Soviet attempts at establishing hegemony over China would be problemmatic.[40] That Stalin intended to be the stronger partner is well known; today, the Russians themselves admit as much. One prominent China specialist has written that Stalin's dealings with the Chinese included "selfless" assistance that was really just a "propaganda trick on our part" and that "Stalin's intention was to build Soviet–Chinese relations on a basis where maximum benefit could be gained for the USSR."[41]

Very little is known about Mao's first visit to the USSR, although many have alluded to his humiliation at Stalin's poor treatment of him.[42] Here he was, the victorious leader of the newly proclaimed Chinese People's Republic, and Stalin snubbed him for several days after a brief initial meeting on the day of his arrival in December 1949.[43] Even this meeting was not a serious state-to-state talk; rather, it was a very general talk to enable Mao and Stalin to become acquainted.[44] The first substantive meeting of Soviet and Chinese government officials did not take place until a few weeks after his arrival.[45] The Soviet press at the time focused instead on Mao's visits to Lenin's tomb or to various prominent factories in Moscow and Leningrad.

Although it is true that the Soviets and the Chinese had a rocky relationship, it is also true that the USSR itself was still recovering from a devastating war and that there were few extra resources in the Soviet economy for China. As we noted earlier, the Treaty of Friendship, Alliance, and Mutual Assistance, which Mao and Stalin signed on February 14, 1950, did not provide for Soviet technical assistance and advice. It only extended credits for Soviet materials to be delivered to China and included a vague statement to the effect that both were to render economic assistance to the other. The treaty granted a Soviet loan of $300 million at 1 percent interest to China; it provided for the joint administration of the Chinese Changchun Railroad until the end of 1952; it laid the groundwork for the Chinese to regain control over Port Arthur in 1952 (for which the Chinese would reimburse the Soviets); and it provided for the return of Port Dalny to the Chinese in 1950.

Nevertheless, it is doubtful that the strained Soviet economy was responsible for its inattention to other, more ordinary details. Traditionally, the Soviet Union had reached out to its client states by publishing a journal in that country's language and by forming a friendship society. It is telling that the Soviets did not bother with either of these tasks until very late in their relationship with the Chinese, thereby demonstrating China's relatively low priority in Soviet eyes. For instance, the Chinese began publishing the Russian language *Narodnyi Kitai* [People's China] in Beijing in November 1950, *Kitai* [China] in January 1951, and the Chinese language *Zhong–Su youhao* [Sino-Soviet friendship] in October 1952. The Soviet counterpart, *Su–Zhong youhao* [Soviet–Chinese friendship], however, was not introduced until January 1958. In a similar manner, the Chinese founded a Chinese–Soviet Friendship Society in October 1949, but the Soviets did not create one until October 1957.

Upon the Communist Party's ascension to power in China, the CCP might have expected that the Soviet Union would send a new ambassador. Again, it seems as if China were a low priority, for the Soviets did not assign a new representative to China. Instead, the Soviet ambassador who was already in China, N. V. Roshchin, remained in Beijing, now as the ambassador to the People's Republic. When the USSR finally did change its ambassador in June 1952, it sent A. S. Panyuskhkin, who also had been the ambassador to Chiang Kai-shek's government, from 1939 to 1944.[46]

The much-heralded Soviet advisers' program through which specialists were sent to build industrial enterprises did not begin in earnest until 1953, although between 1950 and 1952, various Soviet specialists worked in China, particularly in Manchuria under previous arrangements with Gao Gang.[47] Between 1950 and 1953, the USSR also sent various high-ranking Soviets and delegations to tour and lecture in China, but, again, on a very small scale in comparison with China's needs.[48]

One form of assistance that the Soviets did extend to China in the 1949–1953 period was the translation of several hundred Soviet books into Chinese. These were not, however, sources that the Chinese could rely on for concrete advice and plans; they presumably were to aid China in its transition to socialism in general. In truth, as the reader may note, the books that the Soviets chose were more philosophical than practical. From this list, which follows, it would be difficult to gain insight into the mechanics and workings of a socialist economy.[49]

Books the Soviets Translated into Chinese, 1949–1955

Marx and Engels

The Communist Manifesto
Marx's and Engels's *Collected Works* (vol. 1 of 2)

Lenin

Collected Works of Lenin (vols. 1 and 2)
Essays of 1923
On the So-Called Market Question
*Who Are the "Friends of the People," and How Did They Attack the Social
    Democrats?*
What Is to Be Done?
One Step Forward and Two Steps Back
Two Tactics of Social Democracy in the Democratic Revolution
*The Land Program of the Social Democrats in the First Russian Revolu-
    tion, 1905–1907*
Three Sources and Three Parts of Marxism
On Marx and Engels
Critical Notes on the Problems of Nations
The Rights of Nations to Self-determination
Karl Marx (trans. Wei Zhen)
Bankruptcy of the Second International
Socialism and War
*Slogans of the European Federation; Military Program of the Proletarian
    Revolution*
Speech on the 1905 Revolution
The Tasks of the Proletariat in This Revolution
On Marx, Engels, and Marxism
Imperialism, the Highest Stage of Capitalism
The Threatening Catastrophe and How to Fight It
State and Revolution
Marxism and Armed Uprising
Can the Bolsheviks Retain State Power?
Letter to American Workers
The Proletarian Revolution and the Renegade Kautsky
The Current Tasks of Soviet Power
On the State
Great Action; How to Organize a Competition
On the Proletarian Dictatorship
Economy and Politics in the Era of Proletarian Dictatorship
*Report on the Second National Congress of Communist Organizations of
    All Eastern Peoples* (November 22, 1919)

Election of the Constitutional Committee and the Proletarian Dictatorship
"Left-Wing" Communism: An Infantile Disorder
The Tasks of the Youth League
On Unified Economic Planning
On the Agricultural Tax
On the Monopoly of Foreign Trade
On the Cooperative System
On Our Revolution
Less but Better
Critical Notes on the Nationality Question

Stalin

The Proletariat and the Proletarian Party (trans. Wei Zhen)
Marxism and the Nationality Question
The October Revolution and the Nationality Problem
On the Tactics and Strategies of Russian Communists
The October Revolution and the Middle Class
On Lenin
On the Basis of Leninism; on Several Questions of Leninism
The October Revolution and the Tactics of the Russian Communists
Summary Report of the Fourteenth Congress of the CPSU: The Central
   Committee's Political Work (trans. Ya Ping)
Problems of Leninism
The Party's Three Basic Slogans on the Problem of Farmers
On the Soviet Union's Economic Situation and the Party's Policies
The International Characteristics of the October Revolution
Summary Report of the Fifteenth Congress of the CPSU: The Central
   Committee's Political Work (trans. Li Hang)
Three Characteristics of the Red Army
Opposing the Vulgarization of the Slogans of Self-criticism
On National Industrialization and the Right Tendency of the CPSU (Bol-
   sheviks)
The Nationality Question and Leninism
A Year of Great Change
Several Problems of Soviet Land Policies
Summary Report of the Sixteenth Congress of the CPSU: On the Central
   Committee's Political Work (trans. Wei Zhen)
On the Tasks of Economic Personnel; the Tasks of the New Situation and
   the New Economic Order (speech on February 4, 1931)
On the Work of Rural Areas
Speech at the First National Congress of Collective Farm Shock Workers
   (February 19, 1933)
Summary Report of the Seventeenth Congress of the CPSU: On the Cen-
   tral Committee's Political Work

Speech at the First All-Union Meeting of Stakhanovites (November 17, 1935)
Report on the Soviet Draft Constitution—The Soviet Constitution (basic laws)
Two Speeches of the Elective Congress in the Stalin District of Moscow
Dialectical and Historical Materialism
On the Great Patriotic War of the Soviet Union
Economic Problems of Soviet Socialist Society
Summary Report of the Eighteenth Congress of the CPSU: On the Central Committee's Political Work

Society, Politics, and Economics

Lenin and Stalin Are the Great Organizers of the Soviet Union (A. Y. Vyshinsky)
The Great October Socialist Revolution (Moscow: Foreign Languages Press)
The Thirty-second Anniversary of the Great October Socialist Revolution (G. M. Malenkov)
The Thirty-fourth Anniversary of the Great October Socialist Revolution
Thirty Years of Soviet Power (N. Shvernik)
The Soviet Communist Party (Bolsheviks) *Is the Leading Force of Soviet Society*
The Current Right Wing of Social Democracy
The Soviet Socialist State (Moscow: Foreign Languages Press)
The Process of the Soviet Union's Creation of a Socialist Society
Soviet Socialist Society
The Big Unified Family of All Soviet Nations (Moscow: Foreign Languages Press)
The Construction of Soviet Socialist Society (Moscow: Foreign Languages Press)
Nationalization of Soviet Land (Kochetovskaya)
The Soviet Constitution (basic laws)
A Concise Course of the History of Soviet Communism
Disclosing the Fabrications of History (testimony of history and facts) (ed. Soviet Information Bureau)
Soviet National Education (E. N. Medynskii)
On Communist Education (M. I. Kalinin)
Problems of Foreign Policy (V. M. Molotov)
The Soviet Union and the Capitalist World (Moscow: Pravda Publishing House)
Wages of Russian Workers and the Interest of Capitalists
The Great Soviet Patriotic War (Moscow: Pravda Publishing House)
The Role of the Individual in History (G. V. Plekhanov)
Documents and Materials About the Eve of World War II (vol. 1; November 1937–1938) (USSR Ministry of Foreign Affairs)

Documents and Materials About the Eve of World War II (vol. 2; September 1938–1939) (USSR Ministry of Foreign Affairs)

Legal Materials on the Former Japanese Army's Alleged Preparation for the Use of Germ Warfare

Living Conditions of the Russian Workers and Farmers and Their Struggle for Liberation

Methods of Further Developing Soviet Agriculture (resolution, September 7, 1953)

Methods of Further Developing Soviet Agriculture (report on the plenary session of the CPSU Central Committee, September 3, 1953, by N. S. Khrushchev)

Summary Report on Implementing the Fourth Five-Year Plan of 1946–1950 (the first postwar five-year plan) (issued by the Soviet National Planning Committee and the Soviet Central Bureau of Statistics)

Summary Report on Implementing the Soviet 1951 Annual Plan on the Development of the Domestic Economy

Linguistics

Textbook of Russian Language
Chinese–Russian Dictionary
Russian–Chinese Dictionary

Introduction to the Soviet Union

A Revived People (of the Far East) (T. Semushkin and I. Vladimirov)
Karaganda (S. Mukanov)
The Moscow Subway
Skyscrapers in Moscow (A. Vlasov)
The Volga–Don Canal (B. Galaktionov)
The Volga River
Russian and New Soviet Museums
Foreigners in the Soviet Union
What We Saw and Heard in the Soviet Union
This Is What We Saw in Person
What the Scottish Miners Saw
Our Collective Farm
Travels in Tashkent
The Dock Workers of Odessa (B. Smolyakov)
Americans Discuss Soviet Life
The Road to Communism
Worker Committees in the Factories
Sanitoria and Houses of Rest of the Soviet Labor Union
The Workers' Resorts (A. Tret'yakov)

Minsk (P. Abrasimov)
The Palace for Science (G. D. Vovchenko)

Literature and Arts

The Resolutions of the CPSU Central Committee on Literature and Art (1946–1948) (Moscow: Foreign Language Publishing House)

Novels

Day and Night (Simonov)
Death over Subjugation (Gorbatov)
The Key Point (Angelina)

Photos and Picture Albums

Lenin
Long Live Lenin and Stalin
Great Stalin Is the Torch of Peace
We Advocate and Insist on the Course of Peace
We Are Marching Toward Communism
Honest People Stand Shoulder to Shoulder
Lake at Dusk (Yilongkulai Lake)
Picture Collections of Lenin (Moscow: Foreign Languages Press)
Soviet Youth in Pictures (Moscow: Foreign Languages Press)
National Agricultural Exhibit (Soviet National Modeling Art Publishing House)

This list represents what the Soviets thought were most valuable and useful sources for China at the time, but was it really a list of books that would help a poor and backward country create a socialist state? Given the type of books the Soviets sent and the near absence of Soviet expertise and assistance, the Chinese communists themselves selected, read, and translated a list of books that at least appeared to be much more concrete, how-to books. Just in the field of industrial organization and management alone, for instance, the Chinese translated and issued several books with titles such as *Party Control in the Factory*, *The Experience of Political Agitation in the Enterprise*, *Organizational Work of the Production Conference*, and *The Organization of Industrial Management in the USSR*.[50] These are the books that contain the clues to what the CCP wanted and what it found, and it is on these sources that this book is based.

2

The Reality of the Soviet Management Model

In 1949, the Chinese Communists looked toward the Soviet Union for ideas and even a blueprint for China's socialist transformation. As discussed in the last chapter, the CCP chose to study the Soviets' post-war recovery model, which seemed to provide an answer to China's immediate needs and to fulfill two other important functions: It offered a rationale for Communist Party leadership at all levels of management (and society), and it described the methods for training, indoctrinating, and controlling the population. But what exactly was this model?

This chapter examines the USSR's industrial management model of 1946–1950 as it was portrayed in Soviet sources and explains how it actually functioned.[1] This investigation will reveal many aspects of the model that the CCP likely did not know at the time of adoption, since the Chinese communists relied heavily on Soviet written materials and had little firsthand experience with the model. This analysis of the original model will acquaint the reader with the many adverse manifestations of High Stalinism that eventually appeared in China's adapted system.

The model that the Chinese studied and ultimately adopted was more Stalinist than socialist and reflected a bleak period of Soviet history. The CCP learned the particularly intrusive methods of Communist Party control in management, especially in the administering of campaigns and competitions, but perhaps did not fully understand the deleterious effects of these on workers and industrial production alike. The Chinese communists at least appeared to believe in the effectiveness of the Soviet model as a whole and gave no indication that they were privy to the fact that it functioned so poorly that the Soviets privately abandoned the Fourth Five-Year Plan in 1947. Certainly, these many hidden aspects ultimately affected China's development.

The Soviet model was attractive to the Chinese communists for many reasons, but the difficulties of training and recruiting a new labor force particularly interested them. In this realm, the CCP could see many similarities between the Soviet postwar circumstances and the Chinese "postliberation" situation.

The account of labor motivation methods and political indoctrination and control practices is taken from Soviet sources and is supplemented by Western research, so that the reader can see both the exaggerated claims of Soviet successes that the Chinese saw and the actual effects of such methods, which they may not have seen. The next section begins the discussion with the Party's special role in the fulfillment of the Fourth Five-Year Plan.

High Stalinism and the Role of the Party

The period between 1946 and 1950 was an extremely difficult time in Soviet society. At the end of the war, the Soviet Union lay in ruin. Countless regions of the country had been decimated, and many major industries had been destroyed or moved to remote areas.[2] War losses have been estimated at between 20 million and 30 million people. In any case, at the end of 1945, the Soviet population was approximately 2 million to 4 million less than that recorded in January 1939.[3] The Soviets have said that the number of workers and employees in 1945 was only 84.2 percent of the prewar level, and in industry it was 81.5 percent.[4]

Stalin nevertheless had a recovery plan for the USSR. Having won the war, he and the CPSU[5] were infallible: Stalin's will could not be contested. Indeed, Stalin himself made the Party directly responsible for ensuring fulfillment of the Fourth Five-Year Plan,[6] which called on the Soviet people to produce annually 50 million tons of rubber, 60 billion tons of steel, 500 million tons of coal, and 60 million tons of oil. The plan would restore the regions of the country that had borne the brunt of the war, achieve the prewar levels in industry and agriculture, and even surpass the prewar levels by a considerable margin.[7]

Perhaps High Stalinism was the only way to force such a weary population to produce more than the prewar level in such a short time. High Stalinism provided the means, and coercion became the Party's method. The CPSU was, of course, not new to force or intimidation; it had used these methods for years. But, by the postwar period, Stalin was at the absolute height of his power. In his world, he was the ultimate autocrat, and he could not be contested. The Party had often intruded in plan fulfillment, although by the 1939–1941 period, Party involvement in the day-to-day management of enterprises had decreased greatly. The war had thrust the Party back into the thick of daily management operations,[8] and there it stayed for the duration of the Fourth Five-Year Plan.

The Party occupied the dominant position in the enterprise as it carried out its duty of guaranteeing that every worker (including the enterprise manager) fulfilled his or her economic plan. The Party's responsibility for the plan completely threw aside the earlier enterprise management schema whereby the factory manager was in charge of all the factory's administrative activities.[9] This was true for labor management as well as the recruitment and training programs.

In 1949, the Chinese Communist Party was faced with several of the same problems that the USSR appeared to have solved in its postwar period, including ameliorating the shortages of qualified industrial laborers and the lack of skilled industrial workers and solving the basic problem of controlling the labor force. The CCP studied and ultimately adopted many of the High Stalinist methods of recruitment and indoctrination that were used during the Fourth Five-Year Plan. The USSR's labor problems and its solutions in the immediate postwar period are described in the next section.

The Labor Problem in the USSR

Labor Shortages

The USSR's great human losses during World War II meant that at the close of the war, there were not enough workers to reconstruct the national economy. Table 1 illustrates this situation. In 1937, there were approximately 27 million workers and employees in the national economy, and in 1940, there were approximately 31 million. Between 1940 and 1945, however, the number of available workers decreased by 13 percent, or by about 4 million workers, to 27 million. In industry alone, there were about 10 million workers in 1937; 11 million in 1940, and only 9.5 million in 1945 (a decrease also of 13 percent).

Table 1 also shows the results of Soviet postwar mass recruitment programs, the success of which was heralded in the Soviet press. According to these data, between 1945 and 1950, the number of workers and employees in the national economy increased by about 43 percent; in industry, by 49 percent; construction, by 70 percent; and transport, by 63 percent.

Table 1 Changes in the Number of Workers and Employees in
the Soviet National Economy, 1937–1950 (in thousands)

	1937	1940	1945	1950	1945–1950 Growth
Industry	10,112	10,967	9,508	14,144	49%
Construction	1,576	1,563	1,515	2,569	70%
Transport[a]	2,651	3,425	3,111	5,082	63%
Total	26,744	31,192	27,263	38,895	43%

[a]Includes rail, water, and highway transport only.
Source: *Narodnoe khozyaistvo SSSR; statisticheskii sbornik* [The national economy of the USSR; statistical handbook] (Moscow: Gosudarstvennoe statisticheskoe izdatel'stvo, 1956), p. 190.

According to the Administration of Registration and Distribution of the Labor Force (Upravlenie ucheta i raspredeleniya rabochei sily Gosplana SSSR) of the USSR State Planning Agency (known as Gosplan USSR), the Ministry of Labor Reserves (created in 1947) immediately located recruits and funneled them into jobs.[10] The addition of nearly 12 million recruits to the labor force between 1945 and 1950 was the largest increase in Soviet history, with the exception of that during the First Five-Year Plan period.

Demobilized soldiers were the largest group among the new recruits. According to Soviet data, by the end of 1945, 4.5 million soldiers had been repatriated, and by the end of 1948, 8.5 million had been demobilized.[11] Table 2, which illustrates Gosplan USSR's recruitment plan for work in construction, industry, and transport in 1946, shows that demobilized soldiers greatly increased the ranks of workers. Among Gosplan USSR's other sources for labor, including graduates of labor reserve schools, peasants from villages, and students from factory schools, soldiers constituted the largest group. According to Gosplan USSR documents, soldiers were demobilized more quickly and in greater number than originally had been expected.

In 1947, many Soviet industries benefited from soldiers who had been demobilized or repatriated or had returned from evacuation. In the ferrous metallurgy industry, for instance, 25 percent of all the laborers had formerly been involved in the war effort. Many workers in military enterprises were reassigned to civilian enterprises in 1947.[12] But even though thousands of workers were channeled into the appropriate industries through demobilization, repatriation, and transfers, after 1947 the labor needs were still great, due to extraordinarily high rates of worker migration.

The national economy also benefited from a fairly large population of convict and conscript labor in the postwar period. The magnitude of this source is only hinted at in the Soviet sources. For instance, as Table 2 makes clear, Gosplan USSR in 1946 planned to recruit 1.12 million villagers through "organized recruitment," called Orgnabor (the official labor recruiting service, Organizovannyi nabor rabochei sily) to work in industry, construction, and transport.[13] According to the data, Gosplan USSR fulfilled its recruitment plan by only about 60 percent, but was able to add about 100,000 additional workers who were sent "by other means." Each category in Table 2 gained from laborers acquired "by other means."

Sheila Fitzpatrick provides a comprehensive look at this source of labor in the postwar Soviet Union.[14] During this period, the Soviets had two types of convict labor available: its own, including foreigners who had been arrested in the USSR and sent to the camps, and German, Japanese, and other captured prisoners of war.[15] This includes prisoners that were taken during the changes in boundaries in eastern Poland and the Baltic states, as well as in Moldavia, western Belorussia, and western Ukraine; the liberation of Soviets from German-occupied territories, and the punishment of anti-Soviet groups and collaborators. The actual estimates of convict labor remain elusive, however, ranging from 3 million to 5 million to 12 million to 15 million.[16]

Conscript labor is also difficult to estimate. Labor conscription (*trudovaya mobilizatsiya*) was used throughout the war as an obligation comparable to military service, but according to some scholars, the postwar labor shortages meant that it continued after the war as

Table 2   Gosplan USSR's Labor Recruitment Plan and Its Fulfillment for Work in Construction, Industry, and Transport, 1946 (in thousands)

	Labor Reserves	Village (Orgnabor)	Demobilized Soldiers	Factory Schools	Total
Plan	344.9	1,121.5	829.3	39.5	2,335.2
Fulfillment	320.5	669.7	1,338.0	41.4	2,369.6
Percent achieved	93.0%	59.7%	161.4%	104.8%	101.0%
"By other means"	59.8	100.3	182.0	26.6	368.7
Percent "other"	16.0%	13.0%	12.0%	39.0%	13.0%
Total sent	380.3	770.0	1,520.0	68.0	2,738.3

Source: From a Gosplan USSR, Administration of Registration and Distribution of the Labor Force, report on the number and training of workers for 1946. See M. I. Khlusov, *Promyshlennost' i rabochii klass SSSR, 1946–1950; dokumenty i materialy* [Industry and the working class in the USSR, 1946–1950; documents and materials] (Moscow: Nauka, 1989), p. 177.

well.[17] It may be that the designation sent "by other means" listed in Table 2 is conscript labor. If it is, then the nearly 13 percent of those workers sent to work in construction, industry, and transport in 1946 could also have been conscript laborers.

High Worker Migration

Many Soviet industrial ministers complained about the unauthorized migration of workers after the war. Because 1946 was a particularly difficult year, workers moved around on their own, probably owing to poor living and housing conditions and as a result of government "reevacuation" programs. A tally for industrial labor as a whole from Soviet archives shows that in 1946 the percentage of total workers moving from place to place, by quarter, was 6.5 percent, 6.6 percent, 8.0 percent, and 8.0 percent. Certain industries, such as those located in the coal-producing regions in the west, experienced even higher rates. Because of labor shortages, some industries had to reformulate their production plans, and others found they had a great deal of idle time.

In the textiles sector, for instance, the minister noted that the majority of workers who had left textiles enterprises were those who had been there for fewer than one to two years, had come from rural areas, and were young graduates of the FZOs (*fabrichno-zavodskoe obuchenie*, or factory instruction programs) and trade schools (*remeslennoe uchilishche*).[18] Outmigration was also a problem in the construction and railroad machine–building sectors, and ministry officials struggled to curb such movements by workers between 1947 and 1948. The deputy minister noted that in 1947, of the young workers who graduated from the trade schools and the FZOs, 45.8 percent of them had already left their jobs.[19]

This migration of labor continued in the Soviet economy despite official labor legislation that forbade it. The wartime decree by the USSR's Supreme Soviet Presidium of December 26, 1941, stated that if a worker or employee left his or her job, it would be viewed as an act of "desertion."[20] Although the penal stipulations were dropped in 1951, the decree stayed on the books in the postwar period.[21] Western specialists concur that Soviet labor legislation was poorly enforced during this time.[22]

The labor shortages caused by the war and the uncontrollable migration of workers forced the planners to turn to other sources to replenish quickly the ranks of the working class. One solution to this was in the formation of new factory schools, which were created in order to train new recruits and to improve existing worker skills and qualifications.[23] We will discuss the Soviet version of its training programs next, and again, the reader should be advised that it is included because of Chinese interest in it not because it is an accurate account of the postwar USSR.

Training Programs

During the Fourth Five-Year Plan, according to Soviet sources, the government expanded the system of training for newly recruited workers and for those workers who were already employed. The two prewar programs, the schools for professional and technical studies and the courses that were held in the factories, remained in place. The System of State Labor Reserves (Sistema gosudarstvennykh trudovykh rezervev), which was founded in 1940, was the most important government body involved in training workers. This agency was responsible for drafting workers, who were to be trained and were expected to stay at their jobs for a specified period of time. After the war, this agency helped industries make the transition from military to civilian production, by continuing to supply new workers.

Between 1946 and 1950, the Soviets claimed to have trained thousands of new workers and to have improved the qualifications of the thousands who were already on the job. Efforts were made to raise the quality of instruction at both the factory schools and the technical schools and to expand the number of graduates. Soviet sources claimed that thousands of young people were trained at such schools and sent to work in industry.[24]

Table 3 shows that in the first few years after the war, Gosplan USSR carefully outlined the training of new workers and that in 1946, it planned to recruit and train 894.7 thousand new workers. Instead, it was able to recruit about 1.07 million new workers, or about 20 percent more than planned. Again, these increases were probably due to the huge numbers of demobilized soldiers and conscripts. In addition to receiving training in the special schools, some workers were trained "on the job." The main way in which the new recruits were trained was through "individual instruction," but in some industries, such as in the heavy industrial sectors of coal and metallurgy, this was not possible, and so the "course method" was introduced. All of the training was organized by the enterprise itself.

Table 3 also gives the plan levels for improving industrial workers' qualifications on the job. Many workers who were already employed in industry took courses in factory schools to improve their qualifications and to rise in the factory hierarchy. According to the government's perception of needs in 1946, Gosplan USSR planned to improve the training of about 1.6 million workers. According to Table 3, the retraining plans were fulfilled by 99 percent by the end of 1946.

During the postwar period, the Soviet government created numerous "on the job training" programs to alleviate shortages of skilled

Table 3   Gosplan USSR's Labor Training Program in 1946
(in thousands)

Training of New Workers in Industry	Plan	Number Trained	% Plan Fulfilled
Heavy industry	372.9	440.8	118.2
Machine building	210.3	216.4	102.9
Light and foods industries	136.5	192.4	141.0
Construction, building materials, timber, and paper industries	175.0	220.6	126.1
Total	894.7	1070.2	120.0
Improving Industrial Workers' Qualifications			
Heavy industry	451.3	454.9	100.8
Machine building	726.6	670.8	92.3
Light and foods industries	204.9	248.9	121.5
Construction, building materials, timber, and paper industries	190.0	184.8	97.3
Total	1572.8	1559.4	99.0

Source: From a Gosplan USSR, Administration of Registration and Distribution of the Labor Force, report on the number and training of workers for 1946. See M. I. Khlusov, *Promyshlennost' i rabochii klass SSSR, 1946–1950; dokumenty i materialy* [Industry and the working class in the USSR, 1946–1950; documents and materials] (Moscow: Nauka, 1989), pp. 178–79.

workers. According to Soviet sources, between 1945 and 1950, 1.07 million workers were trained in coal industry enterprises, 143 thousand in the fuels industry enterprises, and 48 thousand in the heavy machine–building industry.[25] The majority of this training took place on the job, with "no break from work" (*bez otryva ot proizvodstva*). Unfortunately, there is little indication of the quality or length of such training programs.

Again, the successes of Soviet recruitment and training programs do not necessarily represent the actual situation. In fact, there were grave problems, but they were not discussed in either the Soviet or the Chinese press. Some of these difficulties are described in the next section, which details Communist Party involvement in enterprise management and its methods of controlling and motivating workers.

The Fourth Five-Year Plan: The "Stalin Plan"

According to the official press, the Soviet model in the 1946–1950 period performed extremely well. There were, in turn, many laudatory discussions in the Chinese press about the USSR's successful fulfillment of its Fourth Five-Year Plan.[26] In addition, the Soviets translated their own "Summary Report" into Chinese in 1952.[27] It no doubt looked as if the Soviet Union, in the face of massive labor shortages, had successfully recovered from the war and had rebuilt its economy in just four years. The truth about fulfillment of the Fourth Five-Year Plan is, of course, otherwise, but this was not known in 1949.

Fulfillment of the first year of the Five-Year Plan (1946) cannot be evaluated, since the annual plan itself was never published.[28] Although there was a published plan in 1947, its fulfillment is doubtful. Nevertheless, Western scholars generally agree that the Soviet economic expansion in 1947 was phenomenal.[29] It is thought that because the planners introduced important revisions in 1947, the Soviets actually abandoned the Fourth Five-Year Plan after 1947 and began formulating longer-term plans.[30] The Soviet government nonetheless maintained the fiction of the plan, and attributed all changes to the "unexpected successes" of planning.

According to the Fourth Five-Year Plan documents that the Chinese read, large increases in labor productivity explained the great expansion in production. Behind the increase in labor productivity lay the Soviet postwar methods of mass mobilization, for which the Communist party had responsibility. The Soviet press gave extensive coverage to the "extraordinary successes" of these mobilization methods throughout the 1946–1950 period. No wonder the CCP was so interested in learning these methods.

The next sections examine the party's mass mobilization techniques between 1946 and 1950. Again, the reader should remember that the following sections are based on Soviet writings about this period and that they present an idealized picture of the Party's role. The descriptions of Party methods are of interest here only as a representation of the system that the Chinese communists studied in the early 1950s. The discussion begins with the Party's responsibility for the plan's fulfillment in the postwar period.

The Party's Official Responsibility

Every Soviet source from this period states that the most important goal for all Soviet workers between 1946 and 1950 had to be fulfillment of the monthly, quarterly, annual, and five-year plans. It had always been the Party's responsibility to monitor fulfillment, but from the beginning of the Fourth Five-Year Plan, Stalin had made it clear that the Communist Party was directly responsible for supervising the postwar recovery.

Immediately following the Supreme Soviet's Law on the Plan in 1946, the Central Committee of the Communist Party issued a decree on March 27, 1946: "On agitation and propaganda work of Party organizations in connection with the 'Law on the Five-Year Plan of Reconstruction and Development of the USSR National Economy'," which detailed the Party's "mass-political" responsibilities.[31] This document made clear that the Party at all levels (republican, regional, county, and local) was fully responsible for the performance of each enterprise and factory in its domain.

The responsibility of the Communist Party for plan fulfillment guaranteed that the Party would play an important and visible role at the enterprise level. This, as we noted earlier, was similar to the wartime period of heavy Party involvement in the national economy. The decree itself warned that the Central Committee would evaluate the work of every Party organization on the degree to which it was able to motivate the workers to fulfill and overfulfill the plans.

All Party organizations were immediately instructed to develop a wide-reaching, long-term mass-political campaign to acquaint all workers with the "law" and to explain to every worker that fulfillment of the new Five-Year Plan depended on the contribution of each and every worker. The decree stated that "this is not a short-term campaign but the most important agitation and propaganda work for the near future."[32] The decree ordered that all Party, labor union, and Komsomol (Communist Youth League) organizations institute "socialist competition" at all levels to guarantee results.[33]

Party organizations above the enterprise level (e.g., the county or regional Party organizations) were also held responsible for plan fulfillment, thus ensuring their intrusion as well into the affairs of all factories and enterprises in their regions. The decree instructed them to hold meetings with the workers at the enterprises and to organize lectures, speeches, and meetings devoted to the Five-Year Plan. In the decree, the Party lecturers were even given lecture themes for the workers, which included

> The Basic Tasks of the Five-Year Plan of Reconstruction and De-
> velopment of the USSR's National Economy.
> The Plan of Development for Industry, Transport, and Agriculture.
> Increasing the Material and Cultural Level of the People Is the
> Most Important Task of the 1946–1950 Period.
> The Five-Year Plan of the Union Republics.
> The Basic Economic Tasks of the USSR.
> The Construction of a Socialist Society and the Gradual Transi-
> tion from Socialism to Communism in the USSR.
> The Role of Science in the Struggle for the Further Flourishing of
> the Homeland.[34]

The decree also instructed the Party to use the media extensively. All journals and newspapers were told to print "propaganda articles and materials" as well as stories about progress in various sectors of the economy. The decree stated that every day the media must publish concrete facts and examples to show practical plan fulfillment in all sectors of the economy, to publicize widely the experience of the best workers (*peredovniki*) of socialist competition, and to popularize the best methods of organizing production and the newest achievements of science and technology that ensured increases in labor productivity. It also ordered that "lagging" enterprises and collective farms be "openly criticized" in the press.[35]

Shortly after the ruling on Party participation was circulated, the fifteenth plenum of the Komsomol also issued a decree, which set out the tasks of the youth organization in ensuring fulfillment of the plan. It stated that "under the leadership of the Bolshevik Party," the Komsomol's task was to attract all youth to realize the new Five-Year Plan on the basis of socialist competition. The main goal, of course, was the plan's fulfillment.

In mid-April 1946, the labor union organization published its decree on its involvement in "the struggle for plan fulfillment." According to this document, the labor union was to be the Party's main assistant in the factory and its most important motivator. It was given eleven different, specific tasks. First, because plan fulfillment was the most important task, the labor union was to explain its significance to the workers every day. Second, the labor union was put in charge of socialist competitions at the factories and enterprises. It was to make workers strive toward the goals of high quality products, high labor productivity, and a decrease in costs.

Third, the Central Committee of the Labor Union was to review the competition's progress at their meetings and plenums, to make sure to share the best workers' experiences with other workers, and to ensure that the factory and local committees used the premiums correctly. Fourth, the labor union was to facilitate "rationalizers" to help reformulate the plan to include work innovations as necessary, to popularize their experience, and to introduce quickly their methods to all other workers. Fifth, they were to create conditions conducive to the workers' cultural and technical growth, by regularly holding lectures at their clubs and palaces of culture and by organizing exhibits on new developments in rationalization and labor safety.

Sixth, the labor union newspaper was to propagandize workers' achievements daily. Seventh, the central, county and factory labor union committees were to ensure labor discipline and see that work was completed on schedule. Eighth, they were to control the workers in order to eliminate waste and avoid excess use of materials; ninth, they were charged with creating "Stakhanovite" schools[36] at the factories to use the innovations, by teaching all workers the new techniques. The final two tasks concerned the more typical labor union activities of ensuring that the wage system was properly implemented and maintaining the correct safety and sanitation standards.[37]

In sum, the new decrees charged Party representatives at all levels with the responsibility for ensuring the plan's fulfillment. They gave the Party full authority over the media to propagandize achievements and to exhort workers to produce. Even the Party representatives' lecture topics were mandated in advance. Most important, the decrees firmly established Party control over the enterprise and factory organizations, the Komsomol, and the labor union, in administering the mass mobilization drives the Party was about to undertake.

The Party's "Control" over Economic Activities

The Party and its "assistants" in the factory, the labor union and the Komsomol, were thus charged with responsibility for the plan. What did this mean at the factory level? Although thousands of different types of factories were subject to this type of "Party management," the following account from a small pamphlet by N. Chernyak is a typical description of how one factory Party committee took the lead in the Moscow Transformer Factory's economic affairs in the late 1940s.[38]

N. Chernyak, who was the secretary of the Communist Party bureau, gives a clear picture of Party involvement at the factory level by relating how the factory made the transition from a postwar low level of productivity to one of winning awards in 1947 and 1948. According to his account, once Stalin charged the Party with responsibility for the plan's fulfillment, the factory's Party committee immediately set about investigating any problems that existed in the production process. It assembled a "Party bureau brigade" of about twenty people to look for "bottlenecks" that impeded the production process. According to Chernyak, it did not take long to discover the "bottleneck" workshop. The brigade analyzed the problem, held meetings with communists and specialists alike, and finally came up with some solutions.

The brigade members submitted their recommendations in a draft resolution, which the Party bureau duly adopted. Those who worked in the "bottleneck" workshop immediately received a new, better-defined work program. Chernyak points out that this new work plan was not the only significant part of the solution, for in addition, everybody was now aware that hereafter the factory could no longer rely on old techniques. Immediately following the adoption of the Party resolution, the factory chief engineer called a meeting on restructuring the work of the "bottleneck" workshop. He introduced the Party resolution and began to implement it. Chernyak continues the story, with the resolution's successful implementation.[39]

During the prewar period of enterprise management, as described by Joseph Berliner, the Party–management relationship varied greatly by region or factory and also by the personality of the Party representatives and managers who were involved. In general, since the factory Party committee and the local Party officials all were "dependent in large measure" on the success of the enterprises in their areas, there was a great degree of cooperation between the two organizations. It seemed clear, however, that the plant manager was in charge and leaned on the Party for help in attaining materials and other obligations associated with production.[40]

The Soviet postwar literature depicts a more intrusive role for the Party: Its wartime role was left intact. For instance, the Party was clearly able to suggest changes in factory organization and expect that the administration (in this case, the chief engineer) would implement them. As it appeared in Chernyak's factory, the administration was left with little choice but to follow the Party's recommendation. The same was to be true in the use of techniques of mass motivation of labor, since this was the purview of the Party, as the next sections illustrate.

The Party's Labor Motivation Methods

The Party employed several types of mass motivation techniques in the enterprises, all of which were administered by the Party's two assistants, the labor union and the Komsomol. The most important motivation method was the socialist competition, which is discussed in the next section. The Party and its assistants also encouraged workers to submit "rationalization proposals" and "innovations and inventions" and even to write personal letters to Stalin, in which workers pledged plan fulfillment goals.

According to Soviet sources, shown in Table 4, in 1946, 83.3 percent of all workers in industry, construction and transport were involved in some officially sponsored socialist competition; by 1950, 90.1 percent were involved. Although 90 percent is hard to believe, the nation was nevertheless caught up in a whirl of propaganda about competition.[41] Whether or not the numbers are inflated is not the issue; the important point is that the "competition method" of labor mobilization, led by the Party, was highlighted in all forms of the media as crucial to the postwar Soviet economic recovery. This enormous drive for campaigns, competitions, innovations and other mass methods of labor management caused the factory administrators to rework the plan constantly and no doubt contributed to the decision in 1947 simply to lay the Plan aside.

Every Soviet account of the Fourth Five-Year Plan period emphasizes the important role of the Party in encouraging workers to join the competitions. According to the Soviet sources, the Party "supported the creative initiative of the masses, helped the social and economic organizations and the leaders of production uncover new reserves, and also carried out great organizational, ideological and educational work."[42]

Table 4   Number of Industrial, Construction, and Transport
Workers Participating in Socialist Competitions
in the USSR, 1946–1950 (in thousands)

Year	Number of Workers	Percentage of All Workers
1946	8,715.2	83.3%
1947	9,753.9	84.9
1948	10,220.1	88.0
1949	11,595.3	88.7
1950	12,744.1	90.1

Source: Compiled from Soviet sources and published in *Istoriya sotsialisticheskogo sorevnovaniya v SSSR* [The history of socialist competition in the
USSR] (Moscow: Profizdat, 1980), p. 150.

The Party's duty was hampered in the immediate postwar period,
however, because the war had inflicted great losses on the Communist Party's organization. In particular, the number of primary Party
organizations had declined drastically because of the war.[43] As Soviet
sources express it, after the war, the Party needed to improve "its fighting efficiency" (*boesposobnost'*) by expanding the number of Party
members and Party organizations.[44] More Party members were needed
to supervise the economic recovery and to organize large numbers of
workers in socialist competitions.

A massive recruitment drive was undertaken: Two-thirds of all
Party members in the postwar period had joined during the war.
Cynthia Kaplan found that between 1941 and 1945, the Party recruited
8.4 million members and candidates.[45] This recruiting continued after
the war. According to Table 5, between 1946 and 1951 the number
of communists working in industry, transport and construction grew
by about 71 percent, and the number of primary Party organizations
increased by about 69 percent.

Again, whether or not the numbers in this table are accurate is
not as significant as the fact that there indeed was a drive to increase
Party membership in the postwar period. Perhaps because of the Soviet
experience, the Chinese communists also carried out a Party membership campaign in the early 1950s.[46] From the CCP's reading of the
Soviet literature, it was obvious that the economic recovery required
massive Communist Party guidance.

Socialist Competition: A Lesson in High Stalinism

A typical socialist competition of the postwar period, as described in
Soviet sources, can be seen as the embodiment of High Stalinism. It
was a nationwide, mass movement. Its themes were often indistin-

guishable from those of a military campaign. The competition was carried out and supervised down to the last detail by the Communist Party and its subordinate organizations in the enterprise. This campaign was also meant to educate the workers and to change their worldview through immersion in Marxism-Leninism. Finally, the goal of the campaign, as in a military battle, equated economic recovery with patriotism.

It is not surprising that the Party continued its militaristic campaign style into the postwar period. First, it had been successful during the war. Second, of the 8.4 million Party members recruited during the war, almost 80 percent of them were from the armed forces.[47]

At the factory level, the competition was set up as though it were a battle in which one side "challenged" the other. Under the Party's guidance, a group of workers issued a challenge to another group (or workshop to workshop, factory to factory, etc.) to compete in reaching a certain plan goal. The challenge became a ubiquitous slogan; it would be seen and heard everywhere in the working environment. At the Moscow Transformer Factory, for instance, the factory's Party committee published the challenge in the factory newspaper *Elektrik*, announced the challenge on the plant's broadcasting system, and hung red panels in the workshops with slogans such as "We Will Fulfill the Five-Year Plan in Four Years!"

Table 5   Growth in the Number of Communists and Primary Party Organizations in Industry, Construction, and Transport in the USSR, 1946 and 1951 (in thousands)

Growth	*1946*	*1951*	
	Number of Communists		
Industry	828.1	1,431.2	72.8%
Construction	47.3	102.7	117.1%
Transport	262.4	416.4	58.7%
Total	1,137.8	1,950.3	71.4%
	Number of Primary Party Organizations		
Industry	16.3	27.8	70.6%
Construction	2.1	4.8	128.6%
Transport	10.1	15.6	54.4%
Total	28.5	48.2	69.1%

Source: Istoriya kommunisticheskoi partii sovetskogo soyuza: v 6 t. [History of the Communist party of the Soviet Union: in 6 vols.], vol. 5, book 2 (Moscow: Nauka, 1980), p. 136. Cited by M. I. Khlusov, *Promyshlennost' i rabochii klass SSSR, 1946–1950; dokumenty i materialy* [Industry and the working class in the USSR, 1946–1950; documents and materials] (Moscow: Nauka, 1989), p. 219.

The Communist Party and its subsidiary organizations, the labor
union and the Komsomol, were instrumental in carrying the momen-
tum of the competition. Chernyak explained that the factory Party
bureau created a monthly plan of topics which was then given to the
workshop Party organization, along with a list of literature on the
topics. For the more important political topics, the Party bureau rati-
fied a special plan of speakers who were entrusted to guide the leading factory workers. These speakers were typically members of the
Party bureau, the secretary of the factory Party organization, the director, the chief engineer, the heads of the sections and workshops, and
any engineers with a high level of political training. These kinds of
meetings were held in the workshops every week.[48]

The factory Party committee also prepared the "agitators" (*agitatory*)
or propagandists to supervise, teach and transmit the Party line to the
workers. The "Party agitation collective" at the Moscow Transformer
Factory, for instance, had more than 140 members and was headed
by a member of the factory Party bureau. The Party held two "instruc-
tional meetings" of the entire collective every month, at which the
agitators received guidelines on how to best hold meetings on this or
that topic, listened to speeches, and learned how to solve various
organizational problems.

The Communist Party preached that the success of socialist competition hinged on every worker's level of involvement, awareness,
and "ideological training." It was believed that a solid grounding in
Marxism-Leninism would make the workers understand the importance of their role in the factory, thus compelling them to work harder.
The Party also did not hesitate to communicate to the workers that if
they did not follow its directives, they were being unpatriotic. Several High Stalinist themes are apparent in the following description
of a "typical" meeting during lunch break in a factory welding workshop. We find here the prominent role of the Communist Party representative, the stress on education and patriotism, and the use of military terms to describe the participants.

The day before the meeting, the secretary of the Party organization informed the workers that they should assemble for a meeting.
The welders gathered in the "red corner" of their workshop. The discussion was begun by the production director, who explained that
millions of Soviet people were striving to fulfill the plan ahead of time
and that fulfillment of this plan would strengthen the power of the
state and move them all nearer "to a shining and happy life, to communism."[49] He told them that this work was an example of love for
the motherland and that "life-giving Soviet patriotism" gave birth to
heroic deeds. He reminded them of their pledges to Stalin of the previous year and suggested that they overfulfill their pledge to him this
year.

At this point, Chernyak continues, the agitator took the floor. He explained that there was not one sector of industry that did not rely on the transformers that their factory produced. He related how the Stakhanovite labor of one of the leading workshops (*frontoviki*, "front-line soldiers") also enabled the other workers to become Stakhano-vites.[50] He gave concrete examples and mentioned the names of those who had worked well or who had successfully taught other workers new techniques.

Then a brigade leader stood up to say that the workers all felt that they had to live up to their promise to Stalin. He shouted, to the general agreement of all present, "Could we really not stand by our promises to Stalin? We, the welders, were the first to take on such obligations, and we must be the first to make an example of preplan fulfillment. We can and must do this!"[51] And so went the thousands of accounts of socialist competitions that were readily available in the Soviet press in the postwar period. The pages of newspapers and journals were filled with such descriptions, especially those that detailed the introduction of several new types of competitions. All of the depictions of socialist competitions followed a predictable pattern, and all shared the characteristics of High Stalinism.

The Chinese communists paid a great deal of attention to the summaries of Soviet socialist competitions, whose details later appeared in the Chinese press. Sometimes the CCP even translated the names of famous Soviet Stakhanovites into Chinese, in order to teach the workers the "scientific" methods that they had perfected. A good example of this was the "Kovalyev method," which was widely discussed in the Chinese management literature.[52]

Types of Socialist Competitions in the Postwar Period

The first socialist campaign in which Soviet workers participated during the postwar period was in celebration of the victory over the Germans. According to Soviet sources, the workers who called for this competition (workers at ferrous metallurgy, aviation industry, and machine-building enterprises) proposed that they compete for higher labor productivity, early plan fulfillment, mastery of new types of production, improvement in quality, and decreases in costs. The labor union recommended that this competition be extended to all sectors of industry, and the Komsomol organization immediately suggested that improvements in educational work be included.[53]

The second all-union socialist competition was organized in conjunction with the adoption of the Fourth Five-Year Plan. As we noted earlier, the Party, labor union, and Komsomol were immediately mobilized to guarantee the plan's fulfillment. The Party and the labor union summoned the workers to respond to the challenge, and on May 15,

1946, in *Pravda*, the metallurgists of the Makeevskii Factory (named after S. M. Kirov) responded with their own challenges. Soon the press was filled with numerous workers' pledges.[54]

The third challenge during this period came from Leningrad. In February 1947, collectives of fifteen Leningrad enterprises published their challenge to all others in a Leningrad newspaper.[55] They appealed for all workers to fulfill the second year of the plan by November 7, 1947, which was the thirtieth Anniversary of the October Revolution. According to the Soviet press, these challenges were met.[56]

In 1947, the newspapers also published innumerable "letters to Stalin" in which the workers pledged preplan completion of targets by the thirtieth anniversary of the October Revolution. One letter from a group of coal miners, for instance, noted that they had increased their coal production in 1946 by 10 percent, and in 1947, they promised a 16 percent increase over 1946. A metal worker named Martynov at the Magnitogorsk Metallurgical Works was quoted: "If the amount of steel I smelted last year above schedule was 4000 tons, then the amount I now pledge to produce above my quota this year is 6000 tons."[57]

In line with the March 27, 1946, Communist Party decree, which ordered the media to propagandize daily the labor goals and achievements, one after another of the central newspapers published the competition challenges. The oilmen of Bashkir challenged those in Azerbaidzhan to compete; those in the Volga area challenged those in Groznyi; the iron and steel workers in the Urals challenged those in Ukraine; and the machine builders of Moscow challenged those of Gorky. The major newspapers published spirited commentaries: "A new and powerful wave of socialist competition is sweeping the entire country. At mass meetings and gatherings, at their work benches and machines, the Soviet people express their readiness to surmount the postwar difficulties and fulfill the Stalinist Five-Year Plan ahead of time."[58]

Since the authorities proclaimed that the second year of the plan had been fulfilled ahead of time, the possibility was raised of finishing the entire Fourth Five-Year Plan in four years. Again the initiative came from Leningrad, in a *Pravda* article of November 19, 1947. The idea soon spread across the nation, illustrating a pattern of competition and propaganda that continued throughout the Fourth Five-Year Plan period.

Between 1946 and 1950, the Party was pressed to come up with various new types of competition in order to keep constant pressure on the workers. Most competitions involved collectives, until at one point, the workers of one factory challenged the workers of another factory to compete in fulfilling each worker's personal production plan.

For this purpose, each worker's production targets were calculated in norm hours, and he or she was issued a little booklet, called "Labor Contribution of Socialist Competition Participant" (Trudovoi vklad uchastnika sotsialisticheskogo sorevnovaniya). The booklet contained the norm-hour obligations for the years 1948 and 1949, so that the labor union officials could keep track of each worker's progress.[59]

According to the Soviet sources, many new methods and techniques were discovered in the midst of the competition fever. Again, the reader should remember that this account in no way purports to be actual and indeed represents an idealized picture. It was assembled from the press reports from the 1946–1950 period and is what anybody who followed Soviet economic developments during the Fourth Five-Year Plan might have read; indeed, the Chinese Communists read and wrote extensively about them.

Innovations and Inventions

In the midst of involving Soviet workers in socialist competitions, the Party encouraged workers to try to make better use of machinery and tools. To accomplish this, the Party encouraged each worker to submit proposals to "rationalize" or improve the work regime,[60] as well as to suggest production-related inventions or innovations.

The main initiatives for innovations in the work regime in the Fourth Five-Year Plan period can be roughly divided into five categories: innovations in speed, collective methods, instruction of workers, increases in, quality, and economy and thrift.

The first was known as the "quickest method" technique, which was based on producing at the highest possible rate. P. B. Bykov of the Moscow Grinding Machines Factory established the record: In one year he fulfilled 7.2 years' worth of plan goals. Then G. S. Bortkevich of Leningrad broke a record with his lathe, with a speed that rose from 340 meters a minute to over 800.[61] The second initiative that this period witnessed was to expand from single feats of Stakhanovism to collective Stakhanovite achievements. In 1946, a Moscow shoe factory cutter named V. Matrosov proposed that every worker's work plan be recalculated and set at the rate of shock worker (*udarnik*) and Stakhanovite. This was successfully implemented in his workshop and then introduced nationwide. It was followed by N. Rossiiskii's introduction of this technique on a factorywide basis, to spur the "lagging" workshop of every factory to become a Stakhanovite workshop.[62]

Once the change from individual to collective types of Stakhanovism was pioneered, there appeared to be a need for new teaching techniques. Chief engineer at the factory "Proletarian Victory" F. L. Kovalyev created the third initiative, called "scientific teaching" (*nauchnyi izuchenie*). This consisted of studying the leading workers' most rational methods of executing every production operation and figuring out how best to teach it to the workers. He emphasized worker instruction to improve technical and cultural levels.[63]

Kovalyev's methods gave rise to new ways of teaching workers the most advanced methods. Soon factories everywhere had established "innovators' schools" in their workshops. According to Soviet data, about one-quarter of all workers who improved their qualifications during the Fourth Five-Year Plan studied in this type of school in the factory. In Leningrad, even interfactory and interregional schools for workers were established.

Two Leningrad workers, P. Zaichenko and A. Loginova, submitted a related initiative, for introducing advanced methods on the basis of individual plans, which were created for every worker at his or her work station. The method for checking on the progress of the worker's fulfillment described earlier by Chernyak was undoubtedly part of this campaign.

Fourth, an initiative put forth by A. Chutkikh encouraged workers to produce higher-quality products. Chutkikh worked at the "Red Cotton Worsted Kombinat" in Moscow, and in 1948, 99.5 percent of his brigade's output was high-quality material. This movement was nationwide in 1949, and even the labor union embraced this by issuing a decree.

Finally, at the end of the 1940s, there was a campaign to improve the economy and thrift of materials and resources. This initiative came from the Leningrad shoe factory "Skorokhod" [speedy walker]. A cutter named Ol'ga Mushtukovaya proposed that an account be kept of every worker's use of materials. The mass introduction of a socialist competition came in May 1949, on the initiative of M. I. Rozhev and L. F. Kononenko to reduce the waste products of wool in garment construction.[64]

How did the Communist Party and the labor unions urge the workers to submit such proposals? They were encouraged by the Party's daily speeches at work, by broadcasts on the factory intercom system, and even on the personal level. In some factories, each worker was given a booklet to keep track of his or her labor progress. In Chernyak's factory, the back of the little workbook "Labor Contribution," contained this notice:

REMEMBER: Every factory administration has a special bureau for workers' inventions!

If you can put forth a proposal for rationalizing a work unit, a work process, instrument, or equipment,

If you think that there is something that you or your comrade can do more simply, quickly, or cheaply to introduce some kind of change,

If you have some sort of invention and want to apply it and patent it, even though it does not have a direct relationship to our production,

FILL OUT THE PAGE CALLED "WORKER SUGGESTION"; briefly describe your idea and your proposal (even include a drawing if you can), and give it to the workshop office.[65]

As an outside observer like the CCP might have seen in 1949, it appeared that the Soviet labor and management methods had been enormously successful in prodding workers to fulfill the Fourth Five-Year Plan. The Party was given the responsibility for the plan, and it quickly and responsibly mobilized all available resources. It expanded its own ranks quickly and then engaged an enormous number of workers in socialist competitions over the period. The Party kept the pressure on the workers by initiating various types of campaigns and propagandizing heavily, as well as overseeing the work of each laborer on a daily basis.

Conclusion

The Chinese Communist Party in 1949 knew that recruiting and training laborers would be a key element of China's socialist industrialization. Just as the Soviet Union did after the war, China in 1949 suffered from immense shortages of qualified industrial laborers. In the Chinese case, the number of industrial workers who had been trained before 1949 was miniscule in comparison with the total population: less than 1 percent.[66] This explains the Chinese interest in Gosplan USSR's recruitment and training of laborers in the immediate postwar period.

Even more serious was China's lack of highly skilled industrial workers. This is the reason that the Soviet example of factory training programs and technical schools, which appeared to produce the needed laborers, was a useful example for the Chinese. In addition, the Chinese communists faced the problem of worker control, which appeared to have been solved in Stalin's Soviet Union by a strong Communist Party organization. How else could a very war-weary population have undertaken the massive effort of economic recovery? To an outside observer, like the CCP in the early 1950s, Stalin's solutions were worthy of intense scrutiny.

This chapter examined the High Stalinist model that the Chinese communists studied, emulated, and adopted, including its feature of Party control and a plan that did not work in reality. The Soviets' blueprint for success in the postwar recovery was really a simple lesson: The Party had to be in charge of all activities concerning the plan's fulfillment. This was the lesson of High Stalinism, a management system that turned plan fulfillment into a "battle," complete with the use of military terms; involved heavy CPSU intervention in the day-to-day operation of enterprises; advocated various "mass methods"; emphasized the education and reeducation of all workers in Marxism-

Leninism to inculcate in them the proper "worldview"; and linked economic goals with patriotism.

For the Chinese communists, the Soviet model was attractive precisely because it was both an economic and a political model, even if they did not fully understand it and its workings. They most probably did not have a realistic perception of how the plan worked; they no doubt were not privy to any real data concerning the Soviet economy other than press reports; and they almost certainly were not aware that the Fourth Five-Year Plan had been abandoned after 1947. The Chinese communists could not have fathomed, for instance, the disorganizing effect of socialist competition and Stakhanovism on the production process.

The most important point is that the Soviet Union presented a viable model calling for strong political control by the Communist Party, and it provided the rationale for large-scale political indoctrination (in the course of socialist competitions and other campaigns). The calls to patriotism, the adulatory letters to Stalin, the cajoling and oversupervising of the workers by the Party all produced the desired results. It was an example of mass campaign par excellence, and was a great lesson for the Chinese communist leaders.

3

Soviet Socialism in Translation

In October 1949, a self-proclaimed socialist government took control of China. It was a country so unprepared for socialism that its working class was almost nonexistent. Therefore, one of its first tasks was to begin the process of socialist industrialization and, with it, to create a working class. In order to accomplish this, the Chinese Communist Party turned to the Soviet model of 1946–1950 for methods and techniques. As recounted in previous chapters, the CCP embarked on a major translation program, and soon thousands of Soviet textbooks, handbooks, and journals were available in Chinese. Most of them were products of the period of High Stalinism and therefore contained the five basic characteristics of militarization, Party control of day-to-day management, mass methods, education and reeducation programs, and patriotism.

In the enterprise management literature, which this chapter reviews, strong Party control was the leitmotif, as seen in the USSR's prescribed seven management precepts. The same is true for those books and articles describing techniques for labor motivation and control. This chapter begins with a look at the state of China's working class in 1949, since the formation of a proletarian class was a necessary precondition to successful socialist industrialization.

Problems of Creating a Chinese Working Class

On the eve of its communist revolution, China was a poor, mainly agricultural country suffering the effects of years of civil war and foreign incursion. Its needs were great and immediate: In order to establish socialism in China, the Chinese communists needed to industrialize China's economy and to educate and control its population. The newly established workers' state also needed workers.

In 1949, China's working class relative to total population was very small. As Table 6 indicates, the total number of workers and employees constituted less than 1.0 percent of the total population. Of the 8 million workers and employees, only about 3 million were industrial workers, and only about 10 percent of the country's population resided in urban areas.

In addition to being a miniscule part of the total population, the Chinese working class in 1949 was not organized as a cohesive group. Although the Chinese communists often had attempted to organize workers, the peasantry had been the focus of CCP work before the revolution. The CCP largely failed in its work with the Chinese proletariat; instead, it worked its way to victory by relying on the Chinese peasantry.[1]

In 1949, however, the Chinese communists intended to turn their peasant-backed revolution into a proletarian revolution. This was a difficult task, given the unusual history of the Chinese working class. Even though there is a fairly extensive Western literature on the Chinese working class,[2] Western specialists admit that they have few good explanations as to why the working class was a weak link in the decisive stages of the revolution.[3] Fortunately, our understand-

Table 6   Population and Employment in China, 1949–1953

	Total Population (in millions)	Percent Urban	Workers and Employees (in thousands)	Industrial Workers (in thousands)
1949	542	10.6	7,977	3,059
1950	552	11.2	10,166	3,386
1951	563	11.8	12,705	4,379
1952	575	12.5	15,656	5,263
1953	588	13.3	18,069	6,121

Sources: Total population from *Ten Great Years: Statistics of the Economic and Cultural Achievements of the People's Republic of China* (Beijing: Foreign Languages Press, 1959), pp. 181 and 183; workers, employees and industrial labor statistics from John Philip Emerson, "Employment in Mainland China: Problems and Prospects," in Joint Economic Committee, *An Economic Profile of Mainland China*, vol. 2 (Washington, DC: U.S. Government Printing Office, 1965).

ing of this phenomenon can be supplemented by a well-developed, yet little known, Soviet literature on the subject.[4]

According to Soviet–China scholars, five basic factors surrounding the development of Chinese industry and the working class complicated the CCP's work. First, prerevolutionary Chinese industry was predominantly foreign owned, and foreigners generally held most of the management jobs. Therefore, Chinese workers had little management experience. Second, Chinese industry had not developed evenly across the country and so showed the effects of "regional fragmentation exacerbated by imperialist intervention."[5] Between the 1920s and the 1940s, about 77 percent of all modern industry and factories were located in the coastal regions, with big centers in Shanghai, Tianjin, Guangzhou, and Hangzhou.[6] Industries often depended on powerful warlords for patronage in their regions, and the labor market was therefore regional, not national.

Third, an important consequence of the lack of a unified labor market was that Chinese workers never developed into a distinct "class."[7] In 1949, the nearly 8 million Chinese workers and employees worked in small-scale enterprises.[8] They also exhibited remarkably low levels of mobility, even when working conditions were poor in their region. Because of their relative isolation from other workers, Chinese workers did not develop the feeling of class solidarity or the class goals of unity.[9] Nor could they understand that their poor working conditions and low pay were not caused by one or another avaricious boss or owner but, as the Soviets explained, by "an entire exploitative system."[10]

Fourth, the CCP was not particularly successful in its work with urban laborers, as mentioned earlier, especially in the realm of raising the workers' political consciousness. During the prerevolutionary period, the CCP concentrated on the "national-liberation war," which did not set a national framework for the workers' movement. Therefore, the Chinese proletariat did not form a class consciousness that was separate from its national consciousness.[11] It did not help, either, that about 90 percent of the population was illiterate, and of the workers and employees, about 80 percent were illiterate.[12]

The fifth factor that influenced the development of the Chinese working class was the "gang boss" system in labor management. Soviet scholars characterize this as a "feudal–patriarchal relationship," which implies that Chinese industry did not exist in a clearly capitalist system. It was a system in which a "contractor" (or "foreman") controlled workers for management by hiring and firing them on the basis of highly personal relationships (not the result of a "capitalist" labor contract) with the workers.[13] As Hershatter points out, this system worked because it gave power to the "contractor," who in turn offered his patrons protection or access to better jobs.[14] But there often were gross abuses of power, and at various times before "liberation," factories attempted to undermine the corrupt contractors by changing the system.[15]

The Chinese Communist Party, therefore, faced a difficult task in creating an urban proletariat from a population that had almost no management experience, was spread thinly across China, had never developed into a real "class," had a poorly developed political consciousness, and had not worked in a true capitalist system. The Chinese Communists answered this need to create a working class by adopting the methods of the Soviet postwar recovery plan, which emphasized worker training, motivation, and education at the grass-roots level. The Soviet plan also required strong Party control and guidance at all levels, which went along with the CCP's need to establish its authority and power in Chinese society as well.

The next section presents the High Stalinist enterprise management literature on which the CCP ultimately based its own management system. Again, these management handbooks were part of Soviet domestic propaganda and therefore do not necessarily represent reality. All of them were chosen and translated into Chinese by the CCP.

Soviet Enterprise Management Means Party Primacy[16]

Seven basic principles of industrial organization and management appeared in the Soviet literature in the late 1940s and early 1950s.[17] Of the seven, five of them clearly concern the primacy of Party rule in the enterprise, and two of them pertain to functional operations. The seven principles are divided into two groups, the "Party" and the "administrative" management principles:

Party Principles

1. The primacy of the Party and Marxism-Leninism.
2. The Party's "right of control."
3. One-man management, strengthened by Party authority.
4. Democratic centralism.
5. Wide involvement of workers in production through labor union and youth group.

Administrative Principles

6. A production-territorial system.
7. Cost accounting.

These are the precepts the CCP studied, translated, and discussed in its journals and newspapers.

The Seven Precepts of High Stalinist Management

The first principle of Soviet industrial management was stated explicitly as Party control in the enterprise and called for the enterprise manager to have a strong grounding in Marxism-Leninism. The management texts stated that the political approach to economic problems was best, because only by carefully following the policies of the most powerful force in Soviet society—the Communist Party—could the economy develop successfully.[18] In order for the manager of an enterprise to use a political approach to solve economic problems, it was therefore important that he fully understand the teachings of Marxism-Leninism. Without the theoretical fundamentals, the manager "cannot foresee, and consequently cannot direct."[19] With such knowledge, a manager would better understand his role and the significance of his work, and so, therefore, would the workers.[20]

The second precept, the "right of control," charged the Party with ensuring the plan's fulfillment in the enterprise. Although the factory manager was responsible for selecting cadres and workers, the Party was ultimately responsible for their performance. The "right of control"[21] was the link between management and the Party-sponsored labor union and youth group. The Party's role was, through these organizations, to monitor the progress of workers on the plan, to watch over them constantly in an effort to perfect their technical levels, to urge them to upgrade their skills, and to educate them. The management books stressed that the "right of control" was also a good method for uncovering the enterprise's "hidden reserves," which would enable the workers to overfulfill the plan.[22]

The third precept was known as "one-man management," which meant giving one person full responsibility for fulfilling the plan in each organization or enterprise.[23] Under this system, all workers were directly subordinate to the manager, who was a representative of the Soviet state.[24] During the postwar period, however, the Party was charged with guaranteeing that the enterprise fulfill all ministry directives, and in fact, the manager could rely on the Party to ensure that all workers did their part. Thus, one-man management included a major role for the Party.[25] The manager was responsible for his workers' plan fulfillment, and each worker was in turn responsible for his own work, but the system relied on the primary Party organization's "right of control over the activities of administration," which enabled the Party to take any measures necessary to guarantee the plan's fulfillment.

All socialist enterprises must operate according to the laws of the fourth precept, which was known as democratic centralism and had long been a hallmark of the Party in all of its internal operations. It was the process whereby free discussion was allowed before a deci-

sion was made, but once a decision was reached, all had to support
it. In economic construction, this was expressed in the centralization
of leadership and planning and in the decentralization of operational
management. That is, lower organizations had room to maneuver in
the planning process but had to adhere to the plan once it was made.[26]
Democratic centralism was to be a combination of centralized management from above and the wide application of rights and initiatives
to the local organs of management from below.

The fifth managerial precept was the extensive involvement of
workers in production through the Party-sponsored labor union and
youth group. As the arms of the Party reaching to the masses of workers, the labor union and the Communist Youth League organizations
(the Komsomol) were responsible for offering a communist education
to all workers, for strengthening the workers' socialist attitude toward
work, and for raising their level of political consciousness.[27]

The remaining two Soviet principles of organizational management
did not explicitly concern the Party. The first was known as the production-territorial system. The main administrations of the ministries
were formed only by production specialty (i.e., an amalgam of related
enterprises in the entire country) or by area (an amalgam of enterprises in a given territory). This unified production by gathering under
one ministry all the various related organizations and enterprises. In
addition, every unit (ministry, enterprise, workshop, division, and
brigade) had a director who was fully responsible for his section and
who took his orders only from a higher director.[28]

The principle of cost accounting was the other non-Party precept
of socialist management. This meant that the revenues from the sale
of produced items was to cover all production costs and produce
savings when possible. The state gave the necessary funds to the
enterprise, and the enterprise was responsible for using the money
correctly. The books stressed that the profit was not for the "owner,"
as it was under capitalism, but for "all the people" in a socialist country. The profit was to be reinvested in the country as a whole and
would contribute to the further development of socialism.[29]

As the majority of the Soviet management precepts made clear,
the postwar economic recovery included a major role for the Party
and its subsidiary organizations at all levels of management. Clearly,
total Party control was the first priority, but beyond that, the Chinese
communists needed examples of its practical implementation. They
delved further into the High Stalinist literature to learn about the
actual responsibilities and duties of each factory organization. How
should they create, manage, and shape a socialist labor force? What
should the relationship be between the factory organizations? What
did each organization actually do at the factory? What methods were
most successful in forming a productive labor force? The following

section, which is again based on the Soviet *idealized* account, presents the answers that the Chinese communists found to these questions.

Worker Mobilization and Motivation in the Factory

The management of workers in a Soviet enterprise was shared by three "managerial players": the manager, the primary Party organization, and the labor union. The following sections explain what the Chinese read in their chosen Soviet sources of the late 1940s on the managerial tasks in an enterprise.

The manager (or director)[30] of a factory was the enterprise's chief executive. He was responsible for regulating the use of all the factory's financial and labor resources, and he was also fully in charge of drafting the technical, industrial, and financial plans, the plans for technical progress, and any necessary capital construction. He oversaw all departments in his factory and was held responsible for the factory's overall plan fulfillment, for which he relied heavily on the primary Party organization and the labor union.

The primary Party organization (sometimes called the "Party cell")[31] at the enterprise had both a political and an economic mandate. Its political task was guiding and instilling in the workers a socialist attitude toward labor. Its economic task required it to fashion the work collective into a single unit and to mobilize it to fulfill the Party's plan directives.[32]

In the Soviet enterprise of the late 1940s and early 1950s, the labor union was the Party's most important connection to the masses.[33] The Party–labor union link was seen as the embodiment of the "social character of Party control."[34] The labor union's first two tasks paralleled those of the Party in the enterprise: to assist the Party with worker mobilization and with mass-political work. Only the third task, administration, was the labor union's full responsibility.

All factory organizations shared the tasks of educating, mobilizing, and controlling the workers. They watched over the workers in order to improve their labor productivity and labor discipline; maximize the enterprise's resources, equipment, and materials; increase both the quality and quantity of output; improve the organization of work; achieve a rhythmic style of production; maintain strict technological standards; improve technology; correctly organize labor and wages; reduce production costs; and raise the workers' qualifications. Their responsibilities in the factory can be divided into four main groups: organizational work, mass-political work, mobilization of workers, and administration.

We begin with a description of what the Soviet handbooks called "organizational work," which was the one task that fell only to the Party representatives. Again, this discussion follows the Soviet sources (mostly Communist Party handbooks) that the Chinese translated and read in the early 1950s and therefore presents a highly idealized and not necessarily factual account of enterprise management.

Organizational Work

The primary Party organization was to play a "directional and organizational role" in the enterprise's production process. As we mentioned, its most important directional role, the "right of control," gave the primary Party organization the right and the duty to oversee all economic activities in the enterprise[35] and to "reinforce the productive work by Party and political measures."[36] Above all, it was to guide and educate the masses and to form them into a viable collective for fulfillment of the Party's directives.

Time and again the Chinese readers would have read about the importance of Party work in the enterprise. The various examples given in the handbooks devoted to Party work in industry always stressed the strength of the Party vis-à-vis the management. In one example, an enterprise's primary Party organization was charged with ending its factory's destructive habit of "storming" during the production process.[37] This particular factory was producing 66 to 70 percent of its output in the last third of the month, and the Party wanted to steer the factory back to a normal schedule. The Party thus took various measures toward changing the situation, including the recommendation that a certain workshop boss be fired. According to the handbook, he was ultimately discharged and "was replaced with a communist."[38]

Mass-Political Work

The next task in the factory for all enterprise organizations was known as "mass-political work." It involved all official groups on the factory and was said to be one of the most important tasks of the primary Party organization. This work was designed to strengthen the Party's control and to increase its vanguard role and influence at the enterprise. The "vanguard role" included leading socialist competitions, showing initiative, being inventive, ensuring high labor productivity, propagandizing the work of leading workers and their experiences, and directing the non-Party workers.[39]

Party control over the workers depended on a combination of mass-political techniques. To gain political control over the workers, the handbooks suggested daily education sessions for workers in Marxism-Leninism and communist upbringing. To ensure Party control over production, they advised factorywide and workshop-level meetings, as well as convocations of the Party bureau and Party committee meetings, for Party meetings were the "link" that ensured Party control and the "school for Bolshevik education of the Party members."[40] The handbooks stated that the Party must use all means available to increase its own control over production and to ultimately establish "social mass control."[41] In the production process itself, there must be Party representatives at every level, so that the Party could know the progress of production and the habits of each worker. This could include daily or even hourly control over each worker, as needed.

The Party's mass-political work also extended to life outside the enterprise. The textbooks were replete with examples of this type of activity. Before the beginning of films at the Palace of Culture or at other clubs, stated one textbook, a Party representative would appear to discuss the local enterprise's plan fulfillment progress. The Party was to hold mass meetings in the factory's Park of Culture and Rest, at which they honored the best workers. In the evenings, the agitators[42] were to meet with workers in the Party's "red corners" in the workers' dormitories; they hung wall newspapers there and often encouraged the younger workers to produce small amateur performances that broadcast the enterprise's successes. Outside the factory, agitators sometimes hung banners exhorting people by name: "Comrades Beloded, Chebysh, and Belobrov! To finish the funnel by August 11 is a matter of your honor and heroism. Show examples of Stakhanovite labor!"[43]

The Party also regularly displayed photo showcases of the best workers and workshops or of the winners of competitions. Often the "billboard of leading people" (*doska pochyeta*), which was dedicated to the best workers or the competition winners, was positioned in the center of town or at the town's Palace of Culture. The nearby radio station continuously broadcast news of the enterprises, so that "during any moment of relaxation—in the park, in the Palace of Culture, or in the dormitory—the worker could hear the chronicle of the factory's production successes on the radio." In this way, the Party could permeate every aspect of the laborers' working life and leisure time.[44]

One of the precepts of successful mass-political work was that the primary Party organization understand every facet of the enterprise's production management, so as to be prepared to handle any problem. For instance, the experience at the large Moscow plant called Dinamo demonstrates the Party's close involvement in factory affairs. According to the handbook, the city of Moscow was about to celebrate its eight hundredth anniversary, and the CPSU challenged the factory to produce a considerably higher number of parts (above the planned level) for the construction of new trolleybuses, which were to be given as a present to the city.

According to the account, the factory directors felt that such in-

creases were impossible, but the Party committee "knew better." The
Party called a meeting of the best workers and communists, all of
whom promised to achieve the goal. In the end, the goal was achieved,
and the writer of the example pointed out that this knowledge of
factory reserves was the Party's "strongest weapon" over the factory's
economic activities.[45]

Often a big job required a "mass campaign." For the reconstruction of a major furnace at the Dzerzhinsk metallurgical plant, for
instance, the Party launched such a "campaign." Its work could stand
as a study in Soviet methods of mass-political work. The effort, as
described in the Party handbooks, involved hundreds of people at the
plant. To begin the campaign, the primary Party organization studied
the situation, held innumerable meetings, and hung posters and rib-
bons all around the plant and in the city. They gave lectures on the
significance of the reconstruction, explained the "Stakhanovite"
methods of the laborers, and closely watched each worker for shortcomings. If there was a delay caused by a foreman or worker, they
quickly hung more posters that demanded elimination of the problem. They sent out newsletter "flashes" with the latest information,
constructed a bulletin board that charted the daily progress, and
assembled a photo montage of the best workers. Many agitators went
to the workshops and exacted promises of ahead-of-plan fulfillment
from the workers.[46] In all of these tasks, the Party led, with the labor
union at its side as its faithful assistant.

For its role in mass-political work, the labor union was often called
the "school for educating laborers and for interesting them in the
management of production."[47] The labor union's main mass-political
job was to help the Party carry out its political work with the laborers.
The labor union representatives aided the Party in staging socialist
competitions and following the Stakhanovite movement, helped spread
the experience of innovators, and conducted political and educational
work among the workers.

The labor union also initiated programs to promote communist
education, to strengthen the workers' socialist attitude toward work,
and to increase their political consciousness. This was in response to
Stalin, who was said to have believed that a mastery of Bolshevism
was the best way to manage socialist industry.

Worker Mobilization

The Soviet management handbooks devoted the most attention to the
various and widely used mass mobilization techniques. In the postwar period, the factory Party committee trained and relied on "agitators" to motivate workers to fulfill the plan, and the factory labor union
promoted the use of "production conferences."

Agitators were workers and foremen, communists and noncommunists, who held regular jobs at the enterprise but who also worked among their fellow laborers to further the Party's production goals. Based on accounts from several enterprises and plants in the Moscow area in the late 1940s, agitation work consisted of the following four areas: to raise the workers' consciousness and to strengthen their sense of patriotism and national pride; to improve labor discipline by explaining to workers the Party's, state's, and Five-Year Plan's goals and by propagandizing the work of leading workers; to save money by cutting costs; and to introduce new technology.[48]

What was expected of the agitator in the factory? His first task was to imbue the workers with a sense of Soviet patriotism. He taught them to feel honor in their work and to feel the virtue and privilege of being a Soviet citizen. In the process, he might compare their working lives with those of the workers in America, where, it was said, there was rampant unemployment, no workers' compensation, and the constant fear of losing one's job. The agitator generally took his cues from newspaper editorials and special features in magazines, in order to coordinate them with the prevailing political line.[49]

The agitator's second task was to improve labor discipline, and the recommended method was to hold meetings. He might organize a discussion group around the topics "Personal Obligations of the Worker," "How We Struggle to Increase Labor Productivity," and "Could Every Worker Become a Stakhanovite?"[50] Sometimes in the meetings, according to the handbooks, the workers would be so inspired that one might stand up and demand that he be given individual "norm hours" so he could personally guarantee his own plan fulfillment.[51] The Party also regularly asked the best workers to give speeches as an example to the "laggard" (*otstayushchie*) workers.[52] The less talented (or less disciplined) workers were often a subject at the meetings. One agitator reported that his method of dealing with "laggards" was to lecture them on how important labor discipline was to Lenin and Stalin.[53]

The third task of the agitator was to reduce the cost of production. The main source of cost overruns during this period was waste (*brak*), and so the handbooks suggested that the agitator in a workshop keep an account of all materials and their use by each worker.[54] Another problem was that workers sometimes produced poor-quality goods. In one workshop in an attempt to track down workers who were producing shoddy goods, a certain agitator devised a method of inscribing the workers' identification numbers on each unit, which led to a reduction in the number of poor-quality goods.[55] To increase awareness about reducing costs, the manual also suggested organizing meetings with workers on topics such as "The Value of One Minute of Work Time" or "Struggle Against Losses in the Enterprise."[56]

The agitator's fourth task was to introduce new technology and to assist in its implementation. Soviet workers in 1946–1950 had almost to double their previous production output and to master new technology at the same time. It was up to the agitator to help the workers accomplish this. During the Fourth Five-Year Plan, for instance, one popular innovation was the "complex brigade of improvers and innovators," which was introduced by Moscow mechanic V. Kuznetsov and quickly published in all the Party newspapers. The idea of the complex brigade was to carry out an entire "complex of work" connected with realizing a certain innovation or technical improvement. This was supposed to help speed up the time it took to implement the workers' suggestions for improvements and to help encourage inventors.[57]

The Agitator in the Factory

What did a typical agitator do in the factory? Experienced agitators relied on five main methods: visual agitation; meetings with the workers, oral newspaper reading, personal acquaintance with the workers, and socialist competitions.

The Party handbooks stressed the importance of the first, "visual or graphic (*naglyadnaya*) agitation," in mobilizing workers to fulfill the plan.[58] The written word was considered to be a valuable tool. At a typical factory, the Party published a weekly newspaper, and the individual workshops produced tens of "wall newspapers" (*stengazety*). They also published "crocodiles" (*krokodily*), which satirized the work of lagging sections and workers, "flashes" (*molnii*), which were one-page news briefs with short and succinct messages, and "fighting leaflets" (*boevie listiki*).[59]

The Party had full control over "visual agitation." It was supposed to organize an "artist and poster maker's collective" within the primary Party organization's cultural department.[60] Standards for visual propaganda, whether it be a poster or a slogan, were lofty: It must be of high quality and clearly communicate the "grandiose perspectives of the country's movement ahead."[61] The Party exercised "daily control" over the newspaper editors and also held a monthly meeting to lay out the thematic plan for the factory newspaper. In the feature articles, the Party was to communicate "Bolshevik qualities"[62] through examples of the personal experiences of various workers, in order to show their production initiative and the valor of their work.[63]

The second mobilization technique was simply to hold meetings. A meeting served the purpose of informing the workers of some political goal or campaign; it was an open forum for criticism; it was a way to integrate workers into the plant's activities; and it was a way to inspire workers to work harder. In one typical example, at a workshop meeting to discuss output norms, the agitator encouraged the workers to increase their individual contributions. At one point, when the workshop boss mentioned that a certain furnace's output was no more than sixty-two tons of steel, one workshop agitator stood up and protested. He said: "I am very familiar with the furnace—my own experience is not insignificant—so I ask that you give me the output norm of sixty-five tons."[64]

The third mobilization technique was known as the "oral reading of newspapers," which usually took place during the workers' lunch break or just before or after their shift. The Party organization selected readings from the press and told the reader which parts to stress and how to explain the main points. According to the manuals, the reader must be well prepared both to read ("loudly, expressively, and in a literate manner") and to discuss the topic at hand. This "oral reading" should be so good that it would inspire the workers to read the daily press on their own.[65]

The fourth technique was simply for the agitators to get to know the workers personally. This was to be accomplished in what was known as the "five-minute meeting" (*pyatiminutki*), which were to be held with small groups at the beginning of each of the three shifts. While the agitator told the workers about the preceding shift and about the status of their workshop's plan and target fulfillment, he was also to make a special effort to get to know each worker so as to integrate him or her better into the life of the factory.[66]

The socialist competition was the fifth method of mobilizing workers. According to Stalin, this was "the communist method for building socialism on the basis of the maximum performance of millions of laborers."[67] The socialist competition was first used in a mass campaign in 1929[68] but reached its peak during Soviet industrialization. It was called the "great school of communist education of workers" because in the process of competing, a worker should uncover new moral qualities, strengthen and develop a communist attitude toward labor, and overcome old outlooks and habits.[69] According to the management texts, the socialist competition was important because it enabled the Soviets to attain much higher labor productivity gains than those of the Western capitalist countries. They explained to the workers that this would allow the USSR to overtake the West more quickly.[70]

How did socialist competition work? The agitator, who was called the "fighting assistant of the Party organization," would initiate the socialist competitions because he knew the workers and their capacity. He could organize a socialist competition at any level. Perhaps he would arrange an all-union competition, in which all workers everywhere competed to fulfill or overfulfill their norms by a certain time, or a competition between factories, or within the factory between workshops, sections, brigades, groups, or individuals. The workers could compete for plan fulfillment, increases in product quality, better work organization, or higher labor productivity.

The agitator was responsible for inspiring the workers to compete. He was supposed to keep daily records on the competing workers. One creative agitator devised a method known as the "photograph of the workday." He carefully watched every worker and recorded in a book how they spent every minute of the workday. The agitator then called a meeting to compare the best record with the worst, so that the workers would realize the importance of every minute of the workday.[71] This also was supposed to inspire the "lagging" worker to emulate the best workers.

The best worker might be dubbed a "Stakhanovite," as one who had overfulfilled his production norms by introducing innovations in the work process.[72] This was a high honor, and the Stakhanovites were accorded accolades at the factory. Thereafter, the Stakhanovite worker became part of the agitators' "arsenal," to be used at lectures and as models. Some factories organized meetings called "Stakhanovite Tuesdays" so the model workers could tell the other laborers about their work experience and methods.[73] They also were often put in charge of raising the production levels of lagging workers.

The work experience of the Stakhanovites was widely publicized in the press and on the radio,[74] and the Party organizations even published booklets about these workers for distribution at their factory. Some factories organized "Stakhanovite Schools," at which the model worker was asked to lead classes. In some factories, every time the Party organization discovered a lagging section, they organized such a school to help solve its problems.

The Production Conference

The factory labor union's most important task was to assist the Party in mobilizing workers. Although the union worked with the Party on improving labor discipline and labor productivity, setting up socialist competitions, introducing workshop and brigade cost accounting (*khozraschyet*), decreasing production costs, and increasing the quality and quantity of production, its main contribution was to administer what was known as "production conferences" (*proizvodstvennie soveshchaniya*) with the workers.

The aim of the production conference was always plan fulfillment, or solving any problems hindering plan fulfillment. These conferences (or meetings), which ranged from the factory level to the workshop level, were run by the labor union, but the director (of the enterprise, workshop, or section) was responsible for attending, as well.[75] They were to be used as a forum for involving the workers in production, for eliciting their proposals about the organization of work at the factory, and for criticism and self-criticism. They were often referred to as a "form of Soviet democracy" or a "school for communism."

The production meetings were to follow an official, approved format. Labor union officials were given a "protocol" or a document suggesting how to run the meeting. Information was recorded in a special book so that an account was kept of every meeting. It included the date, time, names of the speakers and their professions, and the subjects of speeches and presentations. And in order to make the most of these production meetings, the labor unions encouraged the administration to supply booklets to each workshop so that the workshop head could note down all suggestions and problems and then their subsequent solutions and fulfillment. These were to be reviewed at the next production meeting.[76]

Along with the primary Party organization, the labor union used the production conference to uncover "hidden reserves" and to improve the work of the "laggards."[77] The labor union was often asked to administer the Party's innovations, like the afore-mentioned "photograph of the workday," which required constant attention to every worker. In another case related by one factory's labor union officials, the labor union required the workers to fill out a form called "My Participation in the Fight Against Losses of Work Time." On the form, the worker gave the following pieces of information:

"Reason for Work Stoppage"
"When Work Stoppage Began"
"When Work Stoppage Ended"
"My Suggestions on How to Fully Use the Workday."[78]

Administrative Work

The labor union had sole responsibility for the work that was called administration. It was the union's task to ensure good working and living conditions for the workers, provide social insurance, ensure that labor legislation was correctly implemented in the enterprise, and sign the collective contracts with the workers.

The labor union organized the resources for housing construction, nurseries, kindergartens, sports, and cultural events. It was also in charge of state social insurance, for which all enterprises were taxed. The labor union formed social insurance councils to ensure that all dues were paid in a timely fashion;[79] to see that the work environment was safe and sanitary; to monitor the work of hospitals, kindergartens and nurseries; and to provide "comradely control" at homes to help sick or injured workers.[80]

The labor union was to oversee the implementation of labor legislation in the enterprise. Every enterprise was required by law to undergo a labor union inspection, which was designed to ensure safety standards. The labor union formed a labor protection committee to provide for these inspections. The labor protection committee also looked into the problems of work schedules, the granting of vacation time, and the proper use of child and female labor.

The "collective contracts," which delineated the mutual obligations of the enterprise administration and the workers (as represented by the labor union) to ensure plan fulfillment, were also the domain of the labor union. These contracts were negotiated annually; however, at the end of every quarter, the labor union was obligated to call a factorywide meeting with the workers. The meetings were called simply to inform the workers about progress on the plan and to remind them of their duties to fulfill their contracts.

Conclusion

China looked to the Soviet Union for help in 1949 but received little in the way of direct assistance until 1953. Instead, the CCP was on its own to pursue its urgent goals of industrialization, socialization, control, and the "creation" of an industrial proletariat. It did this by translating Soviet books: CPSU handbooks, propaganda materials, and journal articles, all of which presented a distorted, idealized picture of "the Soviet model." It was the model of High Stalinism, the return of the "revolution from above," with the Communist Party in charge of and involved in every aspect of life and production.

The strength and power of the Soviet Communist Party in industrial production and management is clear in the Soviet materials that the Chinese translated. The Soviet socialist enterprise, as seen by the Chinese in the early 1950s, was more than a producer of goods. It was the embodiment of Marxist–Leninist ideology; it was the main method by which the Communist Party asserted its control over workers and society as a whole; and thus it was inextricably linked to politics. Indeed, in some ways, its mandate was more political than economic. As seen in this chapter, five of the seven enterprise management principles concerned Party primacy.

The "management team" may have consisted of the manager, the Party, and the labor union, but the power was squarely centered in the hands of the Communist Party and its subordinate organizations in the factory. The Party initiated various techniques and methods to ensure the plan's fulfillment and relied on its agitators and the labor union's production conferences to guarantee results. The Party's "right of control" over all economic and social activities of the enterprise made inevitable its interference in the daily operations of the enterprise. Its job was to ensure plan fulfillment at any cost.

Although the Chinese communists took their lessons from an idealized version Soviet model of 1946–1950, its description provided actual techniques for creating and training a new labor force. These were methods that could easily be adopted and that could help the CCP strengthen its own power. The Chinese communists could easily emulate the militaristic tactics of propaganda; they could see the positive aspects of an intrusive and pervasive communist Party presence, both during and after work; they had concrete examples of how well mass campaigns worked, as in the Dinamo factory example; they could see the Soviet Communist Party's belief in reshaping workers' political consciousness and the indispensable role of the Party in reeducation; and they could read about the benefits of linking economic goals with patriotism. All of these High Stalinist elements indeed turn up in the Chinese version of "the model," as subsequent chapters will illustrate.

4

Industrialization: Managing a Socialist Enterprise

The Chinese Communist Party's first goal in pursuing its "dream of a red factory" was to begin the process of socialist industrialization. The CCP's proposed model was a hybrid of Soviet and indigenous thought and included a Soviet-inspired formal statement known as the "Industrial Management Mechanism," as well as its own movement to "democratize" enterprise management. Because of the plethora of contradictory rules and instructions in this proposed model, it was an unwieldy and unrealistic progam for factory managers to follow.

The CCP's attempt at formulating a model shows its reliance on the Soviets' postwar recovery model, but it also shows its drive to satisfy domestic concerns particularly that of solidifying Communist Party control in industrial enterprises. The formal "Industrial Management Mechanism," for instance, was not a direct copy of the Soviet model but a melding of some of the Soviet principles with other CCP priorities. The "Democratization of Management" movement, which was ostensibly created to teach workers some self-management techniques, also was aimed at attracting support for CCP policies in the factories.

This chapter demonstrates that the basic unifying principle behind both the "Mechanism" and "Democratization" was the High Stalinist principle of strong Party control in factory management. The Chinese communists' drive for Party primacy in management greatly influenced the shape of the CCP proposals during this period. It certainly led the

Party to amplify and expand the management model and guided it in its attempts to supplement the model with new programs of workplace "democracy."

The Dual Approach to Industrial Enterprise Management

The years between 1949 and 1953 were a critical time in China's development. Having taken power, the Chinese communists were thrown into the new role of governing an entire country, instead of merely a base area, and of shaping that country's development of socialism. All around China, CCP members were involved in liberating cities and regions[1] while others were planning the course of China's future economic, political, and social development.

As we have seen, the CCP turned to foreign books and articles for ideas. The Chinese communists were very interested in the Soviet Union's postwar experience, especially in the area of labor force development and management. The CCP thought that it could use Soviet methods not only to begin industrialization but also to create a Chinese urban proletariat. After intense study and a massive translation program, the CCP in the early 1950s introduced what it called China's new "Industrial Management Mechanism."

This program relied heavily on translated materials concerning the Soviet management model. This is not to say that the CCP simply imported the Soviet model, for the Chinese model was composed of ten management precepts, as compared with the Soviet model, which had six.

In addition to the formal model, the Chinese communists introduced several innovations, the most important of which was the movement to "democratize" management. This relied on the experience of the Northeast Communist Party leader Gao Gang, who had amassed some basic management experience before the CCP took power in 1949. Gao's model was a mixture of Soviet practices (including the experiences of jointly managed Soviet–Chinese projects like the Changchun Railroad) and various innovations to the model.[2]

The Democratization of Management movement, which was introduced alongside the Industrial Management Mechanism, was designed to motivate and involve every worker in the life of the factory. It was described in an early Chinese management handbook as an attempt to "give the masses the feeling of participation" in order to develop creativity and energy to improve production.[3] The definition of Democratization of Management included a program of "relying on the masses" by forming a factory management committee (FMC) and a factory employees and workers' conference (FEWC) in each factory, a policy of "democracy under centralized leadership," and efforts to motivate workers by correctly organizing them and raising their class consciousness to make them feel like "masters" (*zhuren*).

The common ground for both the Industrial Management Mechanism and the Democratization of Management program was the central role to be played by the Communist Party. The Industrial Management Mechanism, which had its origins in exaggerated and idealized Soviet postwar sources, reflected High Stalinism's focus on the Party as the dominant force in enterprise management. In China's own Democratization of Management movement, as this chapter argues, the Communist Party was also the most important force, since it was authorized to control the various committees that were to be created as part of the program.

This chapter describes the CCP's adoption of some Soviet techniques and its adaptation of them in the creation of its own management system, as well as the CCP's own Democracy of Management movement. The CCP's dual approach also had dual consequences, as it ultimately prevented the successful execution of a coherent industrial management policy in the early 1950s, but at the same time, it carved out a greatly elevated role for the Communist Party in enterprise management. But before we can discuss these consequences further, we should explain the CCP's proposed Industrial Management Mechanism. The reader should keep in mind that this mechanism is mostly the CCP's early recommendations and that like the earlier discussions of the Soviet model, it is often difficult to distinguish fact from fiction.

The CCP's Industrial Management Mechanism

Most of the Chinese factory management texts and handbooks of the early 1950s introduced the advantages of the Soviet industrial management system and proposed it as the model for Chinese factories. These texts were written either about the Soviet model[4] or written about China using examples from the Soviet model.[5] The following section presents the ten principles of the CCP's proposed Industrial Management Mechanism (*gongye guanli jigou*) of the early 1950s. Six of the ten precepts appear to have been copied almost exactly from the Soviet handbooks that came out between 1946 and 1950: the primacy of the Party and Marxism-Leninism, the Party's "right of control," one-man management, democratic centralism, the production-territorial system, and cost accounting. The other four precepts were CCP additions to the model: socialist competition, a Bolshevik style of management, socialist remuneration, and planned management.

The ten Industrial Management Mechanism precepts are presented next. In order to compare them with the original Soviet management model described in Chapter 3, they are divided into six "Party" principles and four "nonParty" precepts, which also allows the reader to see exactly which precepts were originally Soviet and which were added by the Chinese.

The Chinese Industrial Management Mechanism

"Party Principles" Adopted from the Soviet Model
1. Unity of political and economic leadership and Communist Party primacy.
2. Communist Party's "right of control."
3. One-man management.
4. Democratic centralism.

Chinese Additions to "Party Principles"
5. Party-sponsored socialist competition.
6. Bolshevik style of leadership.

Administrative Principles from the Soviet Model
7. Production-territorial system.
8. Economic accounting.

Chinese Additions to the Model
9. Socialist distribution of remuneration.
10. Planned management.

The Ten Precepts of Industrial Management

The unity of political and economic leadership (*zhengzhi lingdao he jingji lingdao de tongyi*) and Communist Party primacy was the first management precept put forth by both the Soviet and Chinese handbooks.[6] The Chinese, like the Soviets, stressed that politics had the leading role over economics and that socialist economic management was based on the unity of economic and political leadership.

The Chinese manuals used Soviet examples to prove that all economic activity must be subordinated to (*fucong*) Party policy. As proof of the wisdom of this policy, Chinese management specialists Hu Shiru and Liu Wenju claimed that the USSR's major achievements of industrialization and collectivization, its victory over the German Fascists, and its remarkably rapid postwar recovery were possible only because of strong Communist Party leadership.

Like the Soviets, the CCP stressed the importance of political education for all cadres, to ensure that the Party and economic leadership could resolve economic problems from the political point of view. It was the Party's job to teach the cadres. The factory Party committee therefore played a large and important role in the political education of factory cadres. The Party committee, after all, had the ultimate responsibility for and control of the enterprise's administrative work.[7]

The second management principle in the CCP's model was the Communist Party's right of control and correct selection of cadres (*jiancha he ganbu de xuanze*). The Party's "right of control" was one of the most important principles of socialist management. Like the Soviet enterprise of the late 1940s portrayed in the handbooks, this meant that the Communist Party had to check and supervise the progress of all of the workers every day, every week, every month, and every plan period, to ensure that each person fulfilled his or her plan tasks.

The second part of this precept was the correct selection of cadres. Stalin's quotation "cadres determine everything" (*ganbu jueding yiqie*) indicated the importance of this principle. The Chinese manual pointed out that in the Soviet Union, all cadres were selected according to Bolshevik principles and on a political basis, which meant that the main concerns were: "Is he or is he not politically reliable, and are his knowledge and experience right for the job?"

Cadres were carefully scrutinized, the handbooks explained, because they must be widely "respected and cherished" by the masses. In the Soviet Union, they continued, all Party cadres possessed the highest moral and political characteristics; they all were extremely loyal to the cause of communism; and they scrutinized each job for its possible benefits to the country. The authors wrote that the CCP wanted its own cadres to achieve this standard as well.[8]

One-man management (*yizhang zerenzhi*) was the third management precept in the CCP's model. The Chinese understanding of this closely mirrored the explanation found in the Soviet handbooks: All workers must obey the factory manager; the manager must obey a boss above him; and the Party was responsible for guaranteeing that all workers and managers fulfilled the plan.

For the successful implementation of one-man management, the Chinese text suggested the following five rules, which were based on the CCP's perception of the Soviet experience: First, cadres must be carefully chosen, trained, and supervised.[9] Second, every worker's position at work must be precisely stated. The specific powers and duties of the management mechanism had to be clearly defined so as to avoid any irresponsibility by the worker on the job. Third, the leaders and masses must have close contacts. The workers must be encouraged to join in all meetings at the factory and to get involved in all groups. Fourth, the economic leadership must use criticism and self-criticism in order to strengthen popular trust (*weixin*) and to solve quickly any problems at the factory. Finally, all Party and economic cadres must have a good command of technology and production economics.[10]

Democratic centralism (*minzhu jizhongzhi*), long a fundamental precept in Soviet Communist Party life, was the fourth management precept. The CCP copied this concept from the USSR in a straightforward manner and used Soviet examples to illustrate how it was used. The Chinese management handbook said that in the Soviet

Union the centralization of management guaranteed the leadership role of the Party and the Soviet state in economic development. The handbook also asserted that only with democratic centralism could the Soviets have ensured strict discipline, respect for the laws, and fulfillment of all tasks.

In this context, the Chinese handbooks emphasized that unity was the most important characteristic in enterprise management. Unified leadership was necessary to fulfill the plan; all lower-level employees must follow the directions of the higher-level employees; and the higher-level employees must supervise the lower ones. In this unity the CCP could see what it called democracy, because all property belonged to the state and all workers participated in management.[11]

Now we turn to the Chinese additions to the Soviet management model, beginning with Party-sponsored socialist competition (*shehui zhuyi bisai*). This was listed as the fifth precept and appears to have supplanted the Soviet precept of "wide involvement of workers in production through the Party-sponsored labor union and youth group." Although it was not an official management precept in the original Soviet model, socialist competition was an important feature of factory life in the late 1940s, especially during the period of the Stalinist Five-Year Plan.[12] As seen in previous chapters, the Communist Party supervised these competitions and directed the factory organizations that administered them.

In the Chinese literature, the socialist competition had four special characteristics. First, it was a method to motivate the masses to fulfill and overfulfill the enterprise production plan. Second, it was the most rational and most powerful organizational tool for enterprise management work. It encouraged the public enterprises to succeed and the workers to learn by example.[13]

The third special characteristic of socialist competition was its potential to attract new Party cadres from among the best workers. The Soviets had demonstrated that it was a good way to train management cadres and to draw from among the best workers those who could be educated and who later would become managers, assistant managers, and group leaders. Fourth, it was an educational device, a way to teach the masses to form a new "labor point of view." According to the Chinese authors, the educational component of Stakhanovite competitions made these the highest form of socialist competition.[14] The Chinese management books were filled with discussions of various Soviet post-war Stakhanovite competitions, the "successes" of which attested to the importance of this method.[15]

Bolshevik style of leadership (*buershiweikede lingdao zuofeng*) was the second Chinese deviation from the Soviet model in the list of enterprise management principles. This precept concerned only the Communist Party cadres in the enterprises, but it was its inclusion that appears to have ensured tight Party control and power in the enterprise, because it overlapped with the second management principle of the Communist Party's "right of control" (*jiancha*). The Bolshevik style of leadership essentially reiterated the Party's "right of control" as the most important requirement of the Bolshevik management style. Other "Bolshevik characteristics necessary for leadership" were listed as well: to know and understand production, technology, and socialist finances; to give carefully deliberated orders and directives; to demand that workers uphold the law in their fulfillment of directives; and to possess good organizational skills.

Party spirit (*dangxing,* or *partiinost'* in Russian) was introduced as another important "Bolshevik" characteristic that was necessary for Party cadres. This entailed being deeply committed to one's work and to following the Party road in all matters. It meant that Party member had to subordinate themselves to the will of the Party and to the social good. The handbook also noted that the Party cadre should always use criticism and self-criticism as "powerful management tools" to uncover and solve problems.[16]

The next four management principles that were part of the Chinese "Management Mechanism" were simply related to administrative responsibilities and had little to do with the Party's role in the enterprise. The first two, the production-territorial system and cost accounting, were drawn from the Soviet management handbooks; the other two, socialist remuneration and planned management, were Chinese additions to the original Soviet model.

The production-territorial system (*shengchan yiquyu zhi*) was adopted with little modification from the Soviet model. It was defined as a straight-line management system (*zhixian guanlizhi*) in which the director of each workshop (or office or small group) has only one person supervising him, and he obeys the directives of this one boss. Likewise, this director gives directives only to those below him. This system was thought to guarantee strict implementation of one-man management.[17]

The principle of economic accounting (*jingji hesuanji*) was the same as the Soviet "cost accounting." The Chinese version included four parts: First, the enterprise must practice strict economy, reduce costs, and increase savings. Second, the enterprise independently worked to fulfill the plan however it saw best. Third, each enterprise must work to integrate planning and cost accounting in its finances, and fourth, all workers and employees were to be encouraged by awards for their good work.[18]

The next two precepts, the principle of socialist distribution of remuneration and planned management, were not explicitly part of the Soviet model. They were added to the Chinese model probably as elements that the CCP felt necessary to explain to managers and workers who were unfamiliar with the Soviet system. The principle of socialist distribution of remuneration (*anlao jichoude shehui zhuyi fenpei yuanze*) was introduced in the Chinese texts as a fundamental law of socialism. The Chinese quoted Stalin to the effect that "wage leveling" (or wage egalitarianism) was pernicious and had to be eliminated. Basically, this principle stated that every worker must be remunerated for his special skills, his efficiency on the job, and according to the quality and quantity of his output.[19] The precept of planned management (*guanli de jihuaxing*) was also presented as a fundamental tenet of a socialist system and appears to have been simply a justification, based on Soviet experience, of a planned economy and planned management.[20]

These ten elements comprised the model for enterprise management that the Chinese Communist Party advocated in the early 1950s, in pursuit of its goal of industrialization. At the same time that this model was being introduced in texts and discussed in management journals, the CCP was also conscious of the need to gain immediately the support of the enterprises' workers and employees. This obviously would not be accomplished simply by telling the workers that the Communist Party was now in charge of economic affairs and that it would now be the most powerful presence in the enterprise. Therefore, the CCP launched a management campaign called Democratization of Management, which strove to include and interest all workers and employees in the affairs of the enterprise.

Democratization of Management

What was meant by Democratization of Management? According to its most famous proponent, Gao Gang, the purposes of this movement were varied: to oppose bureaucracy; to bring together workers, technicians and staff through the "progressive elements" among them; to centralize the views of the masses so as to solve problems; to raise the workers' political consciousness and change their attitudes toward labor; and to fight against sabotage and wrecking.[21]

The objective of "democratization" was to give the workers the feeling that they were participating in management, in order to "develop their creativity and energy." This would in turn encourage them to improve production and would, one hoped, foster their abilities to manage production themselves.[22] From the CCP's point of view, the Democratization of Management movement would also be a good forum for its other goals of worker socialization and control. It was thought that "democratizing" management would facilitate the creation of a new Chinese proletariat.

In practice, Democratization of Management entailed the formation of new "workers' committees" in the factories: the factory management committee, or FMC (*gongchang guanli weiyuanhui*), and the factory employees' and workers' conference, or FEWC (*gongchang zhigong daibiaohui*). Much of the early Chinese experience with factory management committees came from factories in the Chinese northeast that had been "liberated" by the communists before 1949.[23] After the foundation of the PRC, the Party leader in the northeast region, Gao Gang, emerged as a prominent spokesman for the formation of factory management committees.[24]

The Factory Management Committee

What was the composition of the factory management committee? It was headed by the factory director or manager and included the vice-director, the chief engineer, the chairman of the labor union, and representatives from the workers and/or employees who were elected at the general meeting of the labor union. Officially, the factory management committee was charged with somewhat vague tasks, such as discussing and resolving all problems related to production and management (the handbooks mention, for instance, plan fulfillment, enterprise management, production organization, personnel hiring and firing, wages and benefits) and to oversee and summarize all enterprise work.[25]

All departments (*bu*) in every factory were to create factory management committees, all of which were subject to the same rules. The original rules and regulations on creating the FMCs were drawn up by the North China People's Government. They stipulated that the factory management committee of small factories or of the various parts of a large factory must meet once a week and that the factory-wide FMC must meet once every two weeks. This rule could be adapted to the circumstances of each factory.[26]

In general, the rules regarding the factory management committee were quite flexible. For instance, the manager at the Beijing Peoples' Printing Plant, He Xiaochu, reported that his factory management committee met twice a month. On the eighth day, he pointed out, the most important topic was a summary of last month's work, and on the twenty-third day, the topic was next month's production plan.[27] The Shijingshan Electric Power Plant's director, Liu Yingyuan, in contrast, reported that his factory management committee met once a month and that the members often invited technicians and experienced workers to come along to speak for the workers. Three days before the monthly meeting, every representative was told what would be on the agenda at the workshop level meeting.[28]

The factory management committee's responsibilities thus were broadly construed, and so there was also a factory management committee standing committee, which was the link between the factory management committee and the factory's "mass organizations." Its function was to unify the leadership and to coordinate the work of the administration (*xingzheng*), the Party committee (*dangweihui*), and the labor union (*gonghui*), and its members therefore included the factory director, the Party secretary, and the head of the labor union.[29] The standing committee's specific tasks were to facilitate relations between the mass organizations, to hold meetings and handle daily problems, and to overcome the tendency of each department to act on its own. It also was to help the three sides coordinate their work and prevent each from taking improper actions or acting too independently.[30]

The factory management committee had several purposes, many of which coincided with the CCP's goals of worker socialization and control. All of these stated purposes were aimed at educating workers and changing their behavior:

> To unite workers, technicians and staff "through the progressive elements among them."[31]
>
> To "centralize the views of the masses so as to solve production problems."
>
> To raise the workers' political consciousness.
>
> To change workers' attitude toward labor.
>
> To fight saboteurs and wreckers in the factory.

Much of the factory management committee's work had a strong pedagogic veneer. For instance, at some factories, the FMC organized political study meetings in the evenings three times a week, one of their main purposes being to "centralize the views of the masses."[32]

The Factory Employees' and Workers' Conference

In addition to forming a factory management committee, every factory was to create a factory employees' and workers' conference (*gongchang zhigong daibiaohui*), or FEWC, which was headed by the factory labor union organization.[33] The factory employees' and workers' conference had a "watchdog" function over the factory management committee. It had the authority to listen to and discuss the factory management committee's reports, check the factory management committee's administrative and leadership style, and oversee the factory management committee's implementation of criticism and suggestions.

The FEWC was responsible for electing in each work unit (*danwei*) various production branch primary organizations, such as small production groups or production shifts. Elections to the FEWC were held once a year. Under certain circumstances, when needed, a special election could be held to fill a post. Only elected representatives could serve on the factory employees' and workers' conference. Each representative, as an elected official, was in charge of collecting the opinions of workers, participating in FEWC conferences, and explaining all conference resolutions to the workers.[34] The FEWC was to meet once or twice a month, generally during days off or after work, and the meetings were not to last longer than a half-day. Before each meeting, the representatives were to meet to prepare and discuss the agenda.[35]

Just as with the factory management committee, the rules for creating and utilizing the FEWCs were adapted to each factory's needs. For instance, when the Beijing Peoples' Printing Plant began to implement the Democratic Management Program in 1950, the plant manager decided that all workers and employees at the plant had to study for twenty-five days, to make sure that they all understood the concept of "democracy" in management.[36] By 1951, the FEWC was meeting monthly and was working on the factory's production plan, its labor assignments and work summaries, and a plant reorganization. It also, according to the same director, was handling personnel and appraising salaries and the worker-employees' material benefits, as well as overseeing the plan's target fulfillment and an overhaul of the system of rewards and punishments (*jiangcheng zhidu*).[37]

At the same factory, the FEWC was used as a forum for meeting with the older workers, whom the FEWC members now counseled and criticized. The factory director said that before "liberation" the same workers had been afraid to talk but now that they had learned that that they themselves were the "masters" (*zhuren*), they were speaking up. One old worker commented: "It is as if we all are family members; if there is something to say, we say it."[38]

At the Shijingshan Electric Power Plant, the director Liu Yingyuan, used the factory employees' and workers' conference to solve a problem concerning supplies of coal at the plant. At the FEWC meeting, the Party proposed to the administration that whoever could come up with a rationalization proposal (*helihua jianyi*) to resolve the problem of procuring coal would be rewarded with ten thousand *jin* of rice. The administration immediately organized a "coal study small group" in which all qualified technicians and experienced workers could participate. In this way, Director Liu explained, the Party, the administration, and the workers concentrated their resources, and the workers came up with a solution.[39]

Too Many Committees in the Factory?

Almost from the beginning, the relationship between the factory management committee and the factory employees' and workers' conference was fraught with difficulties. In theory, the FMC was organized to listen to the masses through the FEWC. In this way, both were defined as "workers' organizations." However, those factories that actually instituted the system found out that both were staffed by representatives of workers in the form of Party and labor union officials, and not simply by the workers themselves. Moreover, as one factory manager complained, because of a policy to ensure that the Party, the administration and the workers were always in step (*budiao yizhi*) in factory administration, both the FWC and the FEWC were easily controlled by the most powerful body, the Party, and not by the workers. He complained that the FMCs and FEWCs existed only so that "the leaders' intentions turn into the masses' intentions."[40]

Another factory director reported that after only a year of operation, there were problems with the factory management committee and factory employees' and workers' conference system in his enterprise. In the beginning, the Party, the administration, and the labor union formed a group that met every morning. (In reality, this was an informal factory management committee.) Gradually, the formal FMC met less and less frequently, because the early morning meetings took the place of those of the formal factory management committee. Therefore, it became clear that the meetings were actually just gatherings of the directors of the formal factory groups (actually, a manager and two Party officials), and so the connection with the masses was diminished and finally severed.

This factory director complained also that the factory management committee representatives were continually being promoted to responsible positions in the administration, so that their perspectives differed greatly from the workers', and this meant that the factory management committee's type of representation gradually changed. In his factory, he pointed out, the year after "liberation," the factory management committee's representatives were asked only to "give opinions" or "discuss supplies" and nothing else. Because no more was demanded of them, they began to take a "passive wait-and-see" (*xiaoji guanwang*) attitude, and accordingly, the administrative work fell behind (*luohou*). Consequently, the factory management committee's work also slipped. It turned out that some representatives felt that the factory management committee's main work was to resolve big problems during the time of "liberation," or during the transition to communist rule, and once that time had passed, they felt that there was little work to do and so they basically stopped working.[41]

Perhaps these problems were inevitable in the climate of transition from one system to another, or perhaps the way in which the CCP went about introducing such a mixture of management programs contributed to the committees' problems.

The Party Has the Only Clear Management Role

How did the CCP's Industrial Management Mechanism and the Democracy of Management programs work together? A good measure of turmoil and frustration could be discerned among both Party members and factory managers. Some felt that the workers could not understand what was meant by factory management "democracy" or how it was to be implemented. Roles were confused, and questions arose as to who should do what task in the factory.

Often the only organization that was clear about its role was the Party committee, which then came under fire from other administrative groups in the factory. Already in 1950, Democracy of Management's most famoust proponent, Gao Gang, was quoted as saying that the enterprise Party committee was not the executive body but the "leader of the proletarian vanguard" in the enterprise. He said that although the Party could make suggestions, it could not "act for the manager or replace the system of managerial responsibility."[42]

Other factory managers were uncomfortable because they felt that China should follow the Soviet experience exactly, and they saw no evidence of either the factory management committee or the factory employees' and workers' conference in the original Soviet model.[43] A typical question that arose was "Isn't it contradictory to form a factory management committee while implementing the Soviet system of 'one-man management'?"[44]

In reality, it was very difficult to reconcile the elements of the Soviet model that the CCP promoted with the various innovations that were introduced at the same time. The overall management model that the Chinese advocated during this crucial 1949–1952 period was unwieldy. Indeed, in the plethora of suggestions and innovations, only the enterprise Communist Party could be sure of its primary role in management.

Conclusion

Between 1949 and 1953, the Chinese communists were pursuing their "dream of a red factory" and searching for the best path to socialist industrialization. In order to accomplish this task, the CCP had to contend with the two problems of a large population and a very small proletariat. Its approach to these difficulties reflected the CCP's need not only to industrialize China but also to create, train, and educate a new labor force. Its solution was to adopt not one but two management strategies, which signified its desperate need to establish the Party in the primary position in the factory.

The Soviet Fourth Five-Year Plan as a model for China loomed large in the literature of the early 1950s. It was touted as the perfect model of recovery, as a *People's Daily* editorial on November 7, 1950, the thirty-third anniversary of the October Revolution in the USSR, "The overwhelming superiority of socialism over capitalism . . . is most clearly manifested in the splendid achievements of the postwar economic reconstruction of the Soviet Union, which is advancing toward communism."[45]

The Stalinist management model of 1946–1950 was therefore a significant source of information and inspiration for the CCP between 1949 and 1953. The CCP's reliance on this particular model is reflected in the High Stalinist features that appeared in management soon after "liberation." In its formation of factory management committees, The CCP relied on mass methods of organization, and within the various factory groups, the focus was on educating and indoctrinating the workers. And most important, the FMC system called for a very strong Communist Party presence in factory management.

The CCP adopted six of the seven Soviet precepts and added its own four principles to produce a uniquely Chinese Industrial Management Mechanism. At the same time, it also promoted the Democratization of Management movement. In the confusion of introducing these programs at the same time, the only clear lesson in the new China's industrial management was that the Communist Party had the primary role in factory management.

5

Socialization: Creating a Chinese Working Class

When the Chinese Communist Party took power in 1949, it immediately turned its attention to transforming China into a modern, industrialized, socialist state. One of its first acts, as seen in Chapter 4, was to draw up and circulate a management blueprint for managers in their new roles. The CCP's plan of socialist industrialization would mean not only building new factories and enterprises and implementing a new socialist management regimen, but it would also require an industrial proletariat. Millions of new workers needed to be trained and educated, for they had to learn to work in the new, socialist environment. Therefore, the CCP, in pursuit of its second goal, launched a massive socialization drive, which drew much of its inspiration from the written literature of the postwar Stalinist model.

Many aspects of the CCP's mass socialization[1] program in the 1949–1953 period reflected the adoption and adaptation of High Stalinist precepts. This is not to say that the CCP's approach to socialization was simply a copy of the Soviet model, even though many aspects were similar. But its most salient feature, the stress on Party primacy in management, was also the most important feature of the High Stalinist model. The CCP did pursue its goal of creating a new laboring class but did this simultaneously with the goal of increasing Party control in general. Because of the CCP's domestic needs and the nature of the Soviet sources on which it relied, the balance of Communist Party control and economic efficiency in enterprise management was tilted from the very beginning towards political control.

In its approach to creating a new working class, political control was the leitmotif that ran through all of the CCP's actions. As the Chinese Communist Party actively strove to increase the size of the working class, it took a twofold approach to spreading its message. It introduced its new socialist worldview to all new and old workers, and it undertook major organizational changes in the management structure of industrial enterprises.

The first step was to issue new workers' political handbooks, which explained in detail the CCP's socialist worldview. These little books presented an entire belief system for workers, so that they could understand and embrace the new ideology. The workers began to learn in newly organized political classes at work how to "correctly interpret" their own history and position in China and to appreciate the leading role of the Communist Party. In the new schema, the workers were told that they were "masters" (*zhuren*) in socialist China. These handbooks were the Communist Party's attempt to teach workers the rudiments of socialism as well as to garner support for its rule.

Industrialization and the introduction of socialism demanded much more than simply teaching the workers a new worldview. In order to facilitate the drastic changes that were needed, the structure and organization of industrial enterprises also had to change. The CCP recognized that organizational changes would best augment and encourage the Communist worldview among workers. To this end, the Chinese communists fashioned a new factory hierarchy of authority and administration, which was based in large part on their reading of High Stalinist texts and journals. Each factory and enterprise was ordered to establish a Communist Party branch, a labor union, and a youth organization, all of which would participate in factory management. Just as in the Soviet sources, the Communist Party (with the help of its subsidiary organizations) was to be the most influential partner in this management team.

This chapter examines the Chinese Communist Party program of socialization in the early 1950s, especially the Party's new socialist worldview, which was presented to the workers in the early 1950s. The administrative changes in the factories and enterprises that supplemented the worker socialization program were products of the CCP's explicit program of socialist industrialization and worker socialization, and they also reveal the Communist Party's reliance on the methods of High Stalinism as reflected in the postwar Soviet materials that the CCP read.

A New Worldview for Workers

The Chinese Communist Party's worldview for new socialist laborers was explained most succinctly in the workers' handbooks, which were produced in 1949 and 1950.[2] These small textbooks were issued to labor union representatives, who were to use them in factory political study classes. They were intended to be followed in their entirety as a text, but if necessary, the labor union representative could follow the "short course" of five to seven days. In this case, the lecturer was responsible for

> Explaining the position and responsibilities of the working class in leading China.
> Discussing who had to be overthrown (*dadao*) and with whom Chinese workers should unite (*lianhe*).
> Acquainting the Chinese workers with international reality and thought.
> Explaining labor policies.
> Creating a new labor attitude (*taidu*).[3]

The new Chinese Communist Party worldview for workers is presented in its entirety in the next section. Because the CCP apparently believed that creating a working class meant enlightening the Chinese people about their own past and their own history, all the handbooks began by recounting a new, Communist Party–informed version of past events. This total belief system was designed to discredit the former system and to stress the importance of the Communist Party.

First, the accounts relate the history of exploitation in the old society, describing the lives of the workers in old China in terms that illuminated the misery and poverty of their existence. Exposing their sorrowful past was designed to make the workers want to embrace communism, which the handbooks termed a "nonexploitative" system. With their misery in mind, the workers were then taught about the harmful "class structure" of "preliberation" Chinese society and how Communism would eliminate class altogether.

Once the CCP teachings had inspired "class hatred" and incited the workers to participate in "class struggle," the handbooks went on to explain the essence of "New China" under communism. Here the handbooks presented an idealized image of life under communism, relying heavily on examples of the "utopia" that was life in the Soviet Union. The new worldview started with an account of the old China.

The Bad Old Society

The handbooks typically began the discussion of old China by introducing the concepts of class and class struggle, in order to develop the workers' feelings correctly. Their presentation of the "unfair old society" (*bu helide shehui*) clearly illustrated the injustices of the old system and was designed to make the workers angry. The workers were told, for instance, that although "the world is the creation of workers," in old China the workers always suffered. Their livelihood was productive work, such as digging mines and building factories, which produced products indispensable to society, and they also planted the crops that provided food and clothing. On the basis of such outstanding work, the handbooks stated, workers should be "masters of the world" (*shijiede zhuren*) and should be fairly compensated.

In the "unfair old society," however, the handbooks continued, the situation was just the opposite. The workers had only rotton food; their clothing was thin; and their existence was hellish (*diyude shenghuo*). The landlords and capitalists, by contrast, lived in palaces, wore fancy clothes, ate and drank like emperors, rode through their gates in cars, and lived extravagantly, as if in a paradise (*tiantang*).[4] One handbook began its explanation of the plight of the working class of old China with the words: "Workers Suffer! Workers Suffer!"[5]

In this very simple manner, the handbooks divided the world into two opposing camps of "exploiters" and "exploited." The distinction was simple: The "exploiters" did not have to toil like real laborers, and yet they possessed the tools and the land. In other words, they lived off the labor of others. Anybody who could not be called an "exploiter" was himself being "exploited." The exploited had no tools or land; they lived poorly; and they suffered miserably. According to the handbooks, the majority of the "preliberation" Chinese population fell into the exploited class.[6]

Once this bipolar class system had been exposed, the handbooks then explained the nature of socialism. Here began the descriptions of the Soviet Union's socialist "utopia," toward which China would strive, and of "class enemies," against whom the workers in the new China would "struggle." The concept of class enemies was also very simple: A minority of the people exploited the majority, and this was unfair and so henceforth would not be tolerated. In fact, the handbooks stated, the revolt in China came about because the exploiting class had for so long "sucked" (*xishi*) the working peoples' sweat and blood. This antagonism between the two groups, the workers were told, was called "class struggle."[7]

According to the handbooks, the struggle between the workers and the capitalist class typically began as an economic one, generally in the form of reactions to low wages for workers. Once the workers were liberated, the struggle would move from the purely economic sphere to a political struggle. The purpose of the political struggle was to overthrow the reactionary rule, eliminate oppression, and abolish the unfair system of the class society. The handbooks stated that Chinese workers, like their Soviet counterparts, could not stop there, however. In the USSR, the workers had seized power in an armed struggle and then "created political power." This was the strength of the workers, the handbooks asserted.

In the Chinese revolution, they continued, the situation was different. The people depended on the People's Liberation Army's (PLA) victories to overthrow the reactionary rule and to seize power. From that day on, the landlord class ceased to exist, but the workers and the capitalists must still carry on the struggle. The most important hurdle in the ongoing revolution was said to be "thought struggle" (*sixiang douzheng*), which was the attempt to change the people's old way of thinking. Because it was so difficult to alter the way that people think, the handbooks noted, this struggle would continue for a very long time. The handbooks explained that this continuous "thought struggle" was necessary in order to prevent the landlord and capitalist classes from entertaining thoughts of exploitation, oppression and domination, and to prevent the old society's unfair customs and habits from reappearing.

The handbooks usually devoted an entire section to Soviet society, which was called the "society with no system of exploitation." The Chinese workers were told that the Soviet people were the luckiest people in the world because their society was absolutely free of exploitation. According to this account, Soviet workers had discovered the joy of labor.[8] The handbooks stated that in the USSR, all the workers used modern machinery; all the factories were electrified; the workers ate in public dining halls; and they lived in wonderful public dormitories ("wonderful" in that they all were very modern, tall, well lit, and nicely furnished). The handbooks described the Soviet Union's convenient public transportation, the lovely public parks and gardens, the libraries, and the playgrounds, all of which existed for the workers.[9]

An important part of the new worldview also included the correct interpretation of foreign policy issues. In one handbook, a chapter entitled "Down with the Reactionary Guomindang Government" portrayed the Nationalist Party as the evil enemy of China. It accused the Guomindang of representing feudalism and colluding with imperialists and bureaucratic capitalists. Such reprehensible behavior, according to the handbook, caused China to fall behind and caused the Chinese people to suffer enormously.[10] The handbooks then turned to the Chinese Communist Party's role in creating a new China.

The New China and the Chinese Communist Party

The second part of a typical textbook was designed to give workers a fuller understanding of the "New People's Democratic Revolution," by focusing on class distinctions in Chinese society. In addition, this section was devoted to the importance of developing industry and production, revealing why the proletariat was the leading group in socialist society and why the workers should unite with other groups in society. It also introduced the Chinese Communist Party.

The workers were told that they were the most important group in society. The handbooks stated that the proletarian class was the most resolute, the bravest, and the most selfless class in the struggle for socialism in China because it had suffered years of oppression and cruel treatment. Because the proletariat has such good characteristics (*hao xingge*), it must be the natural leader of the revolution.

Then, in a Maoist deviation from the Soviet model, the workers were also told that until full communism developed in China, the proletariat must unite with all of society's "revolutionary elements," which included peasants, workers, and intellectuals. Uniting with all other classes (excluding, of course, the enemy classes) was the only way to defeat China's enemies and build a new China.[11] Even those who owned private companies had to be allowed to stay in business as before, but just until industry and agriculture developed enough to adopt a socialist system.[12]

But who would lead and guide these disparate groups in society? The Chinese Communist Party, the texts replied, because of its bravery, determination, organization, and discipline, must be the vanguard of the workers. The CCP was the "staff officer" (*canmou bu*) that would lead the proletariat in their class struggle. Only because of this "staff officer" had China been able to establish a doctrine, devise new methods, and make plans, in short, to do everything that was necessary for a socialist victory.[13] Party members, the handbooks observed, must be "more advanced" than the regular workers. Although the workers might want to make a communist revolution, generally they did not have the discipline, nor did they comprehend revolutionary "truths" (*daoli*), as only Communist Party members could.[14]

In keeping with standard communist doctrine, the Chinese workers were told that they had become part of an international socialist community that supported the rise of socialism and communism in China. The handbooks claimed that Communists all over the world warmly supported the CCP's goal of bringing communism to China, eliminating classes, and liberating the proletariat and all people. In this struggle that the whole world championed, the handbooks told its readers, the CCP's bravery and selflessness in the war against the Guomindang and the Japanese stood out. In addition, the workers read, the world Communist community now hailed Mao Zedong as the liberator (*jiuxing*) of all of China.[15]

Once China's history had been correctly reinterpreted and the workers understood the basic concepts of class struggle and the primary role of the Communist Party, the handbooks turned to China's future.

China's Glorious Future

The third section of a typical handbook was intended to give workers a feeling for their position and responsibilities as a class in building the "new China." It continued the theme of "everything bad under capitalism, everything good under socialism." This was an extremely important section of the handbook because the CCP's aim was to socialize the workers and give them a new "labor attitude." At this juncture, the workers presumably understood their historic role and mission and were now ready to adopt a new, socialist labor attitude.

The handbooks continued the bipolar treatment of the world. How were workers treated differently under socialism, as opposed to capitalism? The handbooks pointed out that in a socialist system, all production profits were returned to the economy, which in turn benefited each worker. Under capitalism, of course, the profits simply landed in the capitalists' coffers. But under socialism, the workers owned the means of production, and their money helped build a country that belonged to everybody. In the factory, socialism meant a system that did not exploit (*boxue*) the workers. It was explained that once the threat of exploitation had been completely removed from the lives of the workers, they would feel motivated to work hard. In fact, just as the Soviet handbooks also claimed, Chinese workers would soon find that working to build socialism indeed satisfied both their private and public needs (*gongsi jiangu*).[16]

This is not to say that exploitation would not exist in China in the short term. Since the CCP had mandated that privately owned enterprises would continue to function in the Chinese economy in the short term, the handbooks explained that the workers in such enterprises would have to "temporarily endure" the exploitation of factory owners in order to work and to develop production. However, the books stated, under the new rules, the workers could sign a contract with the capitalist owner, to help prevent the capitalist owner from oppressing the workers and attempting to squeeze as much out of them as possible. The capitalists must recognize that the workers were "masters," and the factory owners would be "supervised and urged" (*duci*) to respect the new government's decrees. This, the handbooks pointed out, was still very different from the policies of the old regime.[17]

For the CCP, carefully explaining the differences between socialism and capitalism was crucial to ensuring that the workers understood how and why to formulate their new labor attitude.[18] They promised that the workers would henceforth toil willingly, for they had become workers and could no longer be referred to as just a "household" (*hukou*), as before. The handbooks assured them that their work would make their lives better, because labor was something glorious and happy. Workers would now begin to study technology and culture at the factory, and this was certainly something they could never have done before.[19]

The Communists understood that the promise of fair wages would go a long way toward helping form the new labor attitude. The handbooks noted that employees henceforth would be guaranteed a minimum wage, and, further, the system would take into account a worker's technical skills and training. This system, called "equal work, equal pay" (*tonggong tongchou*) would grant to all men, women, and youth equal wages for skilled labor.[20]

Another part of the workers' new worldview had to include an understanding of the factory labor union, since the union was so important to the workers' socialization process. The handbooks contrasted the new socialist union with those that were formed under the Guomindang, by pointing out that the latter did not really represent the workers and had even kept them from organizing. The new unions were voluntary, and the representatives were to be elected by the workers, under what was called a "system of democracy." This new concept was defined in the handbooks as a situation in which the minority obeyed (*fucong*) the majority and the lower level obeyed the higher level. In addition, the concepts of criticism and self-criticism were labor union practices that had to be introduced.

The labor union had two functions: First, and most important, it had a political function. The labor union was in the forefront of the fight to overthrow (*dadao*) the Guomindang "reactionaries" and imperialists in industry. Therefore, the unions must organize to support and aid the People's Liberation Army to "destroy the enemies." The second function was economic, to develop production and industry. As the handbooks explained this function to the workers, all workers should voluntarily join the union to work hard, obey the new laws and regulations, respect the PLA (People's Liberation Army), and build the new China. This meant that the workers must attend the labor union classes at work, to raise their political consciousness and thus better understand the new government's policies, oppose selfishness, raise technical and cultural levels, and learn to manage their enterprises.[21]

The handbooks provided an overview of the CCP's thinking in the immediate "postliberation" period, and from them we can see the CCP's aims and priorities concerning the creation of a proletarian class. The handbooks, of course, were propaganda pieces intended to motivate the people to work and to support the Communist Party. They promised utopia: After "liberation," there would be a totally new Chinese society in which there would no longer be landlords, the bad capitalists would work for the state, and, most important, there would no longer be any bureaucrats working for the landlord capitalists. The new government would stand for the interests of the workers and peasants, who would participate in state affairs and work to improve China's economic and cultural life. In the future, the handbooks assured their readers, all Chinese people would live a life of happiness (*xingfu*) under socialism.[22]

Happiness under socialism, however, would not come about simply as a result of reading handbooks. Motivating people to work was fundamental to the establishment of socialist industry in China, and so the CCP also began to explore proposals to alter the structure of industrial management. As seen in Chapter 4, many books and articles immediately appeared with details on what a socialist factory should look like and how it should be operated. From the point of view of socialization, how would these institutions be structured? The CCP writings emphasized the importance of the factory mass organizations.

The Factory Mass Organizations

Because of the CCP's goal of creating a working class in China, many of the books and articles on socialist industry in the early 1950s stressed the importance of correctly establishing a socialist factory structure. In the writings, nothing was more fundamental to the workers' socialization than the factory's Communist Party organization, labor union, and youth group. The role of such organizations was to "unite political and economic work" by "relying on the working class."[23] Their common goals were to improve the working class' political study and consciousness (*xuewu*), to motivate and organize the working class in order to increase output, to raise product quality, to decrease waste, and to improve technology.[24]

One management text pointed out that the whole purpose of the mass organizations was to encourage production, which was an important enough goal that it demanded Communist supervision.[25] Indeed, the factory Communist Party organization was clearly in charge of and responsible for the work of the other two factory groups. As one factory management handbook explained, "Aside from its important supervisory (*jiancha*) work, the factory Party organization also naturally directs (*lingdao*) the labor union, the youth group, and all other social groups."[26]

Both the ideas of "unity of political and economic work" and Party primacy in the factory appeared in the Chinese literature exactly as they were portrayed in the Soviet postwar industrial management literature. As already seen, this highly idealized representation of industrial management, known as High Stalinism, advocated the Communist Party's primacy in management and the infallibility of Party leadership. In the postwar period, Stalin was at the height of his authority and power in Soviet society, and the effect of High Stalinism and of the CCP's reading of that period's propaganda on China's development cannot be overestimated, as will be seen in the next section on worker socialization in the factory.

Worker Socialization in the Factory

Just as the Soviet theoretical literature stressed, in China, the Communist Party branch committee was the most important mass organization in the factory. The Dongbei Party manual of 1947 used the following analogy: "The Party central committee is like a person's head; the province, county, and regional Party committees are like a person's waist; and the Party branch is like a person's hands and feet, without which one cannot work."[27]

The branch committee's work was crucial in that it provided leadership of the masses; it directed the labor union, the peasant associations, the self-defense troops (*ziwei dui*), and the street and village governments; and it developed production and struggled against "bad people" (*huairen*). The branch was the Party's most basic organization; in the factory it directed all other social groups and mass organizations.[28]

The organization of the factory Party committee of every industrial enterprise closely followed the Soviet regulations. According to the rules, a Party branch could be organized in every factory, mine, village, enterprise, street, company of the army, office, or school in which there were three or more Party members. The full body of the committee elected the Party branch committee representatives, who would serve for six months to a year. The number of elected representatives was to be determined by the branch Party members but generally ranged from three to eleven members.[29] Every Party branch elected a secretary (*mishu*), a deputy secretary (*fu mishu*), and representatives in charge of organizational matters (*zuzhi weiyuan*), propaganda (*xuanquan*), and small-group (*xiaozu*) work. These areas of responsibility closely mirrored the Soviet practices of supervision, motivation of workers, and mass-political work, at least as they were set out in the CPSU's post-war management handbooks.

The Party secretary was to supervise the factory's plan fulfillment and all branch Party work, to convene the branch committee and full committee meetings, and to deliver reports on the committee's work to higher-level Party organizations.[30] The representative in charge of organizational matters was responsible for supervising other Party members, keeping the minutes, collecting dues, and directing the small-group meetings. The representative in charge of propaganda was responsible for the Party members' education and propaganda among the masses and for other necessities of the work environment.[31] Recruitment of new Party members was a very important task in the 1949–1953 period.[32]

Just as in the High Stalinist factory literature, the economic plan was central to all factory operations. As the CCP's handbooks stated, the factory Party committee's main task was to strengthen Party thought and leadership in order to ensure that the economic plan was the main goal and to guarantee that the Party, the administration, the labor union, and the youth groups were united in thought and action toward this goal.[33] In the enterprise, the Party organization worked to unify the relationship between economic and political work and to supervise the work of the manager (the administration) in order to fulfill the production plan as quickly as possible. The Party organization's role was quite separate from both the (Soviet-inspired) one-man management system[34] and the work of the (indigenous Chinese) factory management committees.

The Party in the Factory

The Party had four explicit tasks that focused on the workers. The first duty was to propagandize correctly the resolutions of higher Party organizations among all laborers. It was up to each Party branch member to make the workers understand the Party's policy and resolutions. This was called "raising their consciousness," which was necessary to make the workers understand why and how they should fulfill the Party's dictates.The Party's second task in the enterprise was to supervise the workers' political, economic, and cultural life, which entailed a thorough understanding of the workers' opinions and demands. All of the workers' needs were to be handled by the factory Party committee; only the most serious problems would involve higher Party bodies.

The Party's third task involved the rank and file members of the Communist Party. The branch committee actively recruited new Party members, collected dues, supervised and reprimanded Party members, and enforced Party discipline. The Party's fourth task was educational. The branch committee was responsible for teaching its members to study and become familiar with Party policies. They were to ensure that all members read the newspapers and discussed Party documents, in order to improve their own political, cultural, and technical level, increase class consciousness, and improve organizational discipline.[35]

Finally, the Party assumed major responsibility for "mass-political" work, which included educating the workers and strengthening the Party's control. This work, sometimes called "thought reform," became a serious part of the CCP's mandate in the factory. It was not a new concern among Communists; Soviet postwar scholars had also emphasized its importance. Political propaganda and the role of ideas in society were major topics of discussion during the postwar period, and the Chinese translated several of the books that informed this debate.

One of the most important of these books was the work of the much-published F. V. Konstantinov,[36] who preached that the political revolution was just a quick maneuver but that the revolution in the people's way of thinking was a long, slow process.[37] Old habits, attitudes toward work, and social mores all were formed under another social system, he wrote, and therefore were deeply ingrained in popular consciousness. These all were hostile to socialism and were the "greatest danger to the existence of the dictatorship of the proletariat." Stalin called them "dangerous enemies of socialism," thus elevating their eradication to a societywide struggle. This, said Konstantinov, was why the Party must devote enormous attention to the Communist education of the masses against the "survivals of the old society."

Konstantinov wrote that art and literature must play a big role in molding people's consciousness so that the rules of Communist intercourse became a habit. Art and literature have one important purpose, he stated, and that is to express socialist ideas, because they can "influence the human mind" in a way that simple ideology cannot. Art and literature not only affect the people's reasoning, but their feelings, and emotions also can influence people's conduct, their social life and activities. That is why these must be placed at the service of the masses and must be accessible to all.[38]

The Chinese communists also took seriously the task of "remolding" the people's consciousness. Immediately after "liberation," they began to stress the role of the propagandist, and so teaching propaganda became a serious vocation.[39] The CCP, like its Soviet counterpart, also recognized the importance and utility of art and literature in workers' propaganda, which appeared as early as 1949 in Chinese factories.[40]

There was so much to teach the workers once China had embarked on the socialist path. The most fundamental work was carried out at the factory level by the factory propaganda network (*gongchang zhongde xuanchuanwang*), which was responsible for resolving "thought problems" among the workers. The CCP propaganda books taught that the "thought problems" (*sixiang wenti*) could be rectified by educating the workers in the ideology of Marxism–Leninism–Mao Zedong thought. The workers must understand that the CCP was the indispensable leader in all areas of Chinese life and that there must be unity of thought between the workers and the Party. This process of politicizating the workers led to the formation of one standard, unified interpretation of the world and its structure of power and authority. At the factory level, the propagandist had to ensure that workers knew and understood that the "USSR was our friend and elder brother" and to introduce them to the concept that patriotism was linked to production.[41]

To teach the workers all these lessons, the CCP followed the Soviet practice of organizing campaigns. The Chinese press covered widely many of the Soviet postwar campaigns.[42] In the early 1950s, the CCP initiated its own version of campaigns: "Increase Production and Practice Economy," "Fight America, Aid Korea," "Suppress Counterrevolutionaries," and "Land Reform." Even the industrial management journals joined the fray. For instance, the November 1950 front cover of *Zhongguo gongye* [Chinese industry] was emblazoned with two slogans:

> "Resist America Aid Korea!"
> "Protect Our Homes and Defend Our Country!"

By May 1951, these had changed to read:

> "Strengthen the Force of the Resist America
> and Aid Korea Campaign!"
> "Firmly Carry out the Work of Resolutely Eliminating
> Counter-Revolutionaries!"

Just as the Soviet campaigns had demonstrated, the campaigns had important political socialization as well as economic functions. As one Chinese propaganda handbook noted, work on the people's consciousness must be continuous; the people must keep in their minds at all times the leading role of the Party.[43]

Campaigns appeared to be the perfect vehicle for relaying the regime's messages, for in a campaign, as the Soviets stressed in their management books, production could be linked to a national goal, and in this way, it became unpatriotic not to produce, which could be a very serious offense. In the early 1950s, the war in Korea was one important national goal. The propagandist could imply that if a worker did not work satisfactorily, perhaps he was responsible for any poor performance in the war.

The Party handbooks stressed that every factory propaganda network must establish and follow a system. The system included regular Party meetings, at which the propaganda goals were announced to the propagandists and their work was divided into specific tasks. At the meeting, the Party should listen to the propagandists' reports (*huibao*) on the state of the workers' thoughts. Then a two-week plan must be devised for propaganda work. The Party must also penetrate all workshops and implement control (*jiancha*). Finally, it must work within the "Party secretary responsibility system," in which the branch Party secretary was the immediate director of all factory propagandists, especially in the area of "thought reform."[44]

The propaganda methods suggested in all Party handbooks adhered to Soviet techniques and included oral propaganda, in which the propagandists formed a close relationship with the workers. The propagandists were around to talk to the workers during all breaks at the factory. One major difference from the Soviet technique was the Chinese suggestion that the propagandists encourage workers to "vent their grievances" and to "recall the past and contrast it with the present" in their meetings. Chinese propagandists were told to follow another Soviet method, that of reading to the workers from the press and other CCP publications. They were instructed to use blackboards, wall newspapers, radios, charts, and posters to reach the workers. Finally, they were urged to organize cultural recreation for the workers so that they could teach the Communist Party's lessons to them after the workday had finished.[45]

The task of socialization, of forming in workers a new worldview, was quite large and could not be carried out by the Party alone. For this reason, the Party also had to help create and maintain a good working relationship with the factory's labor union and youth group. This pattern of factory organization could have been found in any Soviet publication about factory management in the postwar period. Again, the factory organization materials that the CCP produced, like the Soviet counterparts, were idealized and did not necessarily reflect reality.

The Labor Union in the Factory

The factory labor union[46] was regarded as the official mass organization of the working class. The labor union had two broad areas of responsibility. The first was to work as an arm of the Party in the factory to motivate and educate the workers. This entailed supervising the work of the factory employees' and workers' committees and administering the socialist competitions and emulation campaigns. The second area of responsibility concerned social insurance, labor protection, and the signing of collective contracts.

According to labor union regulations, every production or administrative unit with at least twenty-five workers and employees should form a labor union primary representative committee. If the unit had more than five hundred workers, they could form departmental or work-unit committees, as well as small groups.[47]

The labor union's most important socialization tasks required that it work under the leadership of the Party and higher labor union organizations to educate and organize the broad masses, to raise their level of class consciousness (*xuewu*), and to form a new labor attitude.[48] All the handbooks stressed the importance of the labor unions' socialization work. As one Chinese commentator pointed out, if the union's work is not carried out correctly, then "the new labor attitude cannot be established; labor fervor cannot be increased; and the labor union cannot foster the idea that the workers are masters."[49]

Once organized, the factory labor union was advised to set up committees focusing on ten areas.[50] First, it should form an organizational work committee (*zuzhi gongzuo weiyuanhui*), which would manage and direct the development of labor union officials, discover and foster (*peiyang*) labor union activists, keep labor union activities running smoothly, submit monthly plans, and convene monthly meetings, followed up by a monthly report to the labor union primary committee. Second, the production committee (*shengchan gongzuo weiyuanhui*) should motivate the workers and employees to fulfill and overfulfill the production plan, conserve national resources and electrical energy and fuel, increase production, lower costs, take care of the tools and machinery, initiate and oversee production competitions, strengthen labor discipline, and resolve production and wage problems.

Third, there must be a culture and education committee (*wenjian gongzuo weiyuanhui*) that would specialize in propaganda, cultural study, technical study, political study, arts and literature, clubs, libraries, movies, radio broadcasts, and children's education. The most important task was to organize mass participation in after-hours (*yeyu*) educational classes and recreational activities; to improve political, cultural, science, and technology; and to create a new labor attitude. Only when these goals were reached could the production plan be fulfilled or overfulfilled.

Fourth, the committee on living conditions (*shenghuo gongzuo weiyuanhui*) should create a dormitory small group, a group meals group, a sanitation supervision group, and a cooperative group. The most important task was to supervise the building of dormitories and other facilities; to renovate the surroundings; to help formulate dormitory management rules; to participate in dormitory allotment work; to take part in the meetings on the cooperative and public dining halls, barbers, and public baths; to assist in resolving the difficulties of the masses' living conditions; and to help with the women's and the families' committees.

Fifth, there must be a labor insurance committee (*laobao gongzuo weiyuanhui*), which should divide its work into small groups to propagandize the benefits of labor insurance, to care for the ill and wounded, and to supervise hospital affairs and the centralized labor insurance affairs. The committee's most important duties were to propagandize and register labor insurance, to investigate the issuance of labor insurance on first request, to ensure that the adminstration paid its labor insurance bills, to assist in improving hospitals and hospital service, help select model workers (*laomo*) and combat heroes of production (*shengchan zhandou yingxiong*), to judge the cause of accidents, to determine the level of difficulty of jobs, to manage the secretary of the small labor insurance groups, to work out the monthly work plan, and to hold meetings to report on work done.[51]

Sixth was a committee for inventions and rationalization proposals (*faming yu helihua jianyi gongzuo weiyuanhui*), whose main duties were to recruit and motivate workers to participate in inventing and submitting rationalization proposals, working out a monthly plan, and holding meetings and reporting on work done. Seventh was a wages committee to study wages in the enterprise, to investigate any incorrect wage application forms, to assist in measures to rectify the determination of technical norms, to ensure that the grades of work were correct, to supervise the enterprise's carrying out of the government's rules and regulations on wages, to ensure that the wage fund and the plan were in order, and to hold meetings to report on work done.

Eighth, the committee on women (*nugong gongzuo weiyuanhui*) would supervise and ensure that the labor union paid attention to women's issues and special women's benefits, motivate and educate women to participate in production competitions and cultural and technical study, look for ways to resolve all women's problems at work, and encourage and urge women workers in the labor union to take an active role in all labor union activities.

Ninth, the committee on property (*caiwu gongzuo weiyuanhui*) was to coordinate the activities of the examining committee that would oversee each labor union organization's funds, and supervise the leadership of the property committee. Each labor union should have a property department, directly led by the labor union primary committee. Finally, tenth, the committee on family and family members (*jiashu weiyuanhui*) should organize the education of families of the masses, hold family and labor union meetings, and ensure that the workers fully completed the production plan.

Although almost all of the labor union's tasks involved some amount of worker socialization, as can be seen in the description of the committee's work, the committee on culture and education had the explicit mandate to educate the workers. In 1951, a literacy campaign was organized and administered by the union, but even before that, the labor union was involved in teaching the workers to read and write. The political message that the workers were supposed to absorb determined what words the workers learned in their lessons.

One book, for example, which was prepared for the labor unions to use in classes for workers who were barely literate, was organized around the themes "We Are Workers," "Workers Want to Study,"

"Studying Makes Us into Masters," "Workers Are Masters," "Workers Have Been Liberated," and so on. The text was typically printed in big characters and included lessons in writing common words.[52] Another began with a chapter entitled "Workers; Workers Work; Workers Become Masters" and contained a chapter called "We All Love to Work; We Are All Becoming Masters." It ended with lessons that taught workers that a knitting factory was considered to be "light industry" and that a machinery factory was part of "heavy industry."[53]

The political message that the workers were given in the early 1950s can be summarized by an endnote in one volume of the *Workers' Cultural Textbook*. The influence of High Stalinism was obvious, from the stress on Communist Party control, worker education, and mass methods, to the calls to patriotism. The note observed that now that the workers could read, they now could understand that the following was true:

> Labor is glorious.
> We want to study well and produce well.
> We understand that the USSR is our friend; it helps us strive for liberation. We also understand that the American imperialists are our biggest enemies; they want to enslave China.
> In the revolutionary movement, the working class stands in the forefront of the struggle.
> The labor union is the organization of workers and employees; it is run by the workers and employees themselves.
> We now know three or four commonsense rules of sanitation.
> We are now able to write notices, announcements, and introduction letters.[54]

Educational work, to the extent that it was effective, was paramount to the new labor attitude. The Soviets also spent a great deal of time fostering the correct attitude toward labor and labor discipline, and by 1950 many articles describing their techniques and experience had been translated into Chinese.[55] For instance, the CCP's method of keeping a work "diary," which was borrowed from Soviet techniques, was to teach the workers how best to organize their work time. The Chinese version described a month in which the worker begins to study, attends meetings, participates in socialist competition, takes part in criticism and self-criticism meetings, and so on, as his attitude toward the new China and toward work (and his work performance) improved.[56] "Work budgets" that were supposed to help the labor union ensure that all workers were being used to their fullest capacity were also regularly printed in journals and handbooks.[57]

The Communist Party's socialization work in the factory was so extensive that it relied not only on the labor union but on other "helpers," such as the youth group organization.

The Youth Group

The youth group was called the "workers' mass political organization." It was often also referred to as the Party's most "dependable assistant" (*zhushou*)[58] or, sometimes, as the Party's "reserve army" (*houbei jun*).[59] This meant that the Party was in charge of training and fostering the leaders of the youth movement. The youth group's tasks were divided into three areas: ideology, motivation, and administration.

Its first task entailed assisting the Party and the labor union in educating both the members of the youth group and all young workers, to raise their political consciousness—the youth group was sometimes called the "school of Marxism, Leninism, and Mao thought"— and to help them form a correct outlook on life (*rensheng shi*). The youth group also had as its mandate actively carrying out thought reform (*sixiang gaizao*) work with all young workers.

Its second task was to increase production. The youth group must work to develop in all young workers a sense of production activity, creativity, and shock work, by actively participating in and promoting socialist competition, by enabling the young workers to learn from others' advanced production experience, by exceeding the old production norms, and by working to increase the number of rationalization proposals and the number of workers becoming model workers.[60]

Increasing production involved many activities, for instance, the organization of after-hours study groups to teach the workers about culture and technology and the launching of a new movement called "respect the teacher and love the apprentice," to encourage the workers to learn from and respect more advanced workers and to improve relations between the neophytes and the experienced workers.

The third task demanded that the youth group be concerned with the workers' health, that it develop a physical culture movement and cultural recreation movement. It must pay attention to youths' special characteristics and direct their correct handling of life-style problems.

The youth group used many techniques, including drama and art, to reach the young workers. As we have seen, this was considered an important tool among Soviet experts, and the CCP followed their example.[61] It relied heavily on the example of Soviet youth work. Not only were the textbooks, journal articles, and newspaper accounts imbued with examples from the Soviet Union, but also an entire book dedicated to the role of Soviet youth was introduced to workers in 1952, entitled *Soviet Youth Forge Ahead Under Communism*.[62]

Conclusion

The socialization of Chinese workers, a main CCP goal in 1949, was central to the realization of the CCP's "dream of a red factory." One aim of mass socialization was to inculcate China's workers with socialist ideas and norms of behavior, which would spur them to work harder and produce more. Its other important objective was to shore up support for the Communist Party that had so suddenly taken power in China. The very manner in which the Chinese communists went about instituting their program of worker socialization in the factories reflected both the CCP's own concerns with solidifying the Party's power and its reliance on the High Stalinist literature of the 1946–1950 period for methods and practices.

The main message in both issuing political handbooks for workers and rearranging the factory administrative structures was the important High Stalinist premise of Party control. Thus the handbooks recounted all of Chinese history and reconstructed it in a way that would encourage workers to support the Party's leading role. In much the same way, the new factory hierarchy made the Party responsible for the work of the labor union and the youth group, as all three concentrated on worker education and reeducation. Although the Communist Party's control was the main Soviet premise to surface in the CCP's socialization work, all the other High Stalinist elements were present as well. The mass approach to the socialization and education of the new working class, for instance, was not a new idea, but one that had been a focus in the postwar Soviet Union. There were debates, as seen in the work of Konstantinov, about the necessity of eradicating the old ways of thinking. Stalin had already called attention to these by calling them "dangerous enemies," and this was more than enough reason to emphasize worker socialization programs.

In the Chinese case, Stalin's sanctioning of reeducation and "remolding" of the people's consciousness enabled the CCP to rationalize its programs of "thought control" and "thought struggle" among the masses. The CCP had had some experience with educating its members during the Yenan period and, in subsequent periods, in its rectification campaigns.[63] The High Stalinist literature, however, provided actual methods and practices, which, at least as seen in Soviet propaganda, appeared to have been successful. Soviet beliefs about and methods of educating the masses in order to create better workers thus enriched and legitimated the CCP's actions.

China's involvement in the Korean War facilitated the use of the two High Stalinist tenets of militarization and patriotism. As we saw, the Communist Party was in charge of workers in the factories and, in this capacity, was often called the "staff officer." Production was a struggle, after all, and this justified the work of the Communist Party's "reserve army," the factory labor union. Once the war started, then it was easy for the Party to call for increasing production in the name of the war. The offense of lagging in production was tantamount to showing a lack of patriotism, just as it had been in Stalin's postwar economy.

The High Stalinist literature thus was extremely important to establishing patterns of legitimacy for the CCP in the factories. It provided the Chinese with a general organizational pattern for factories, even if the original sources presented a highly idealized version of socialist industrial management. It also gave the Chinese communists their most important organizational feature, the establishment of firm Communist Party control over factory management and over the workers.

6

Control: Manipulating the Masses

The Chinese Communist Party's third goal in 1949 was simply to establish its control over industrial production and over all workers. The CCP's understanding of the Soviet Union's postwar experience largely shaped its policies on and ideas about industrialization and socialization and, similarly, its aim of political control. Based on the Soviet literature, total Party primacy in the factory was seen as the only method that would guarantee overall Communist Party control of enterprise management and administration. The CCP's writings during this period indicate the influence of High Stalinist principles, as reflected in industrial management, which were intense Communist Party involvement in the day-to-day management of industry, the development and use of mass methods, the militarization of management, the belief in worker education and indoctrination, and the linking of economic goals with patriotism.

The creation of mass organizations cemented Party control in the industrial enterprises.[1] This was the Soviet solution so evident in the postwar period, and based on the High Stalinist literature that the CCP translated and read, this also became one of the CCP's goals in the early 1950s. Through the mass organizations, the Party could involve millions of people in campaigns that had ostensible economic goals but whose actual intent was to ensure political control over the participants.

Communist control in factories and enterprises was established through mass organizations. This does not mean control in the formal sense, as described by Franz Schurmann in his treatment of the development of control commissions and "people's control correspondents,"[2] or the high incidence of the Public Security Bureau's involvement in factory management.[3] Instead, we shall examine the Party's efforts to change the population's conception of politics and, indeed, of itself. The Chinese Communists' campaigns were administered by the factory's Party, labor union, and youth group organizations, and they involved all workers. Their goal was to change the workers' outlook on labor and the CCP and to establish Party control over factory life. The latter, as we will see, quickly took on a life of its own.

A mass campaign, according to a Chinese definition, is an "organized mobilization of collective action aimed at transforming thought patterns, class/power relationships and/or economic institutions and productivity."[4] Indeed, an important reason for creating mass organizations, especially those in industrial enterprises and factories, was to transform peasants into workers, who would fulfill the CCP's most basic responsibility of ensuring the plan's fulfillment. To this end, the CCP ceaselessly recruited people to fill out the ranks of the labor union, the youth group, and the women's groups,[5] all of which were involved in almost continuous mass campaigns between 1949 and 1953.

The way in which the CCP used mass campaigns between 1949 and 1953 is revealing, for it illuminates several changes in scope and intent as the political climate changed over time. In the beginning, the campaigns had an economic focus, such as the "Stop Waste" drive, but they quickly escalated into blatant political campaigns that focused on the Party's "class enemies," as evidenced in the Three- and Five-Anti campaigns. This is a clear example of the inevitable changes that adopted structures of organizational management and emulated patterns of institutional authority generally encounter and that reflect other experiences, such as Meiji Japan's transformation in the 1870s. It is also indicative of the Party's role in using these adapted structures for its own purposes.[6]

The following sections describe the work of the mass organizations as the Chinese communists mandated it, the Party committee's focus on the workshop level and its emphasis on "agitation and propaganda," and the labor union's and youth group's preoccupation with socialist competitions, emulation campaigns, and model workers. Throughout the discussion, the reader will recognize the influence of High Stalinism in the CCP's work among the laborers.

Mass Organizations in the Factory

Several Western studies of the earliest period of the PRC point to the importance of the mass organizations. In his Tianjin study, Kenneth Lieberthal notes Liu Shaoqi's early emphasis on them as links between the revolutionary government and the masses.[7] In his study of Canton, Ezra Vogel found that in this early period when the government did not yet directly manage the internal affairs of enterprises, the members of the mass organizations were indispensable to checking the power of the enterprises' leaders, and the newly formed labor unions were used to oversee the work of factory managers. Vogel concludes that "although mass organizations are found in all periods, their power reached a height in this early period before the Party itself took over the managerial role and the role of mass organizations declined accordingly."[8]

The organizational structure of most mass organizations followed a similar pattern. According to a close observer, in the early 1950s all mass organizations had the following basic organizational structure:[9] First, every organization was subordinate to CCP leadership. Second, all groups operated in a quasi-military fashion, with iron discipline and loyalty, all designed to translate for the masses the ideas and precepts of the organization's leader. Third, each operated under the belief that there was only one correct way to act and think and that this interpretation must be taught to and followed by the groups' members. Fourth, each group stressed the necessity of activism. It was not enough simply to belong, one must actively participate in the group's aims.

Each group had a hierarchy, so that members could rise in the ranks, and instructions traveled from the top to the bottom. The most basic unit was the small group, on which the CCP concentrated its attention. This forum was the best for both control and indoctrination. The Party–mass relationship was stressed as the most important link, and all the handbooks were quite explicit about the Party's tasks in the factory.

The enterprise Party committee was crucial to cementing the CCP's overall political control. It had to take charge of all other organizations, be responsible for the plan, and establish Party control over the workers. To accomplish this, the Party relied on its helpers, the factory's labor union and youth group. The following section explores the Chinese sources on the work of the enterprise's Party organization as it strove to establish total Communist Party control, as mandated. This is followed by a discussion of the supporting role of the labor unions and youth group, as they too worked to solidify the CCP's control. Again, the reader should remember that this discussion is based on written Chinese literature and does not necessarily reflect the actual situation in all factories and enterprises at the time.

Party Control in the Factory

The CCP's industrial management model, like the Soviet theoretical model on which it was based, insisted on the primacy of the Party and the importance of its supervisory role in the factory. Even though the CCP may have insisted that all of the mass organizations were equal, the enterprise Party organization was clearly the most important. This was the most prominent High Stalinist characteristic and reflected the Soviet postwar practice that relied on "political" (i.e., Party) leadership over administrative management. According to a basic Chinese management text, the enterprise Party organization had several supervisory tasks in the factory.[10]

In an industrial enterprise, the Party's main task was to ensure the correct formulation and quick fulfillment of the factory's production plan. The Party committee was to see that the factory director and the chief engineer correctly set the plan targets. Once the plan was conceived, the Party organized competitions in all workshops and departments, to make sure the plan was fulfilled. Likewise, it was up to the factory Party committee to see that state laws, decrees, and Party policies and resolutions were carried out and that the workers' collective contracts were strictly observed. The Party committee was in charge of supervising these tasks, and the factory's labor union and youth group carried them out.

The Party committee was also responsible for "democratic management" and for overseeing cadre work. As we found earlier, advocating both one-man management and "democratic management techniques," such as the factory management committees, created confusion, but the Party committee's place in the hierarchy was clear. The handbooks explicitly stated that it was the Party's task to place itself in the middle of the two "management mechanisms" while making clear that the factory's performance was ultimately the Party's responsibility.

The Chinese Communist Party committee, like its Soviet counterpart, also was responsible for choosing, assigning, educating, training, and employing the factory cadres.[11] Higher-level Party and administrative organizations (*dang zheng jiguan*) were in charge of appointments, removals, and transfers of all administrative cadres, but it was up to the factory Party organization to understand and supervise their work. The CCP had read the High Stalinist literature on this subject, and the Soviet methods were clear. As Chapter 3 pointed out, for instance, the Soviets were adamant about what to do with an uncooperative workshop boss: He should be "replaced by a communist."[12] According to the CCP handbooks, the factory administrators' only association with cadres was that they compiled the cadres' employment materials and data, which were turned over to the Party organization for its guidance (i.e., so the Party could decide whether to hire or fire the person in question).

Finally, the Party's job was to spur workers to produce and to encourage and supervise inventions, so as to improve production technology continuously. During the socialist competitions this was especially important, it was said, because workers often offered new inventions and innovations. The Party must support the workers' rationalization proposals (*helihua jianyi*), praise and disseminate the new experiences, and correct any old work habits. In the case of a new method or experiment proposed by an exemplary worker, the Party should strive to implement the new method immediately, preferably in a single day, and make sure that each worker learns it. It was up to the factory management (generally the chief engineer) to convene technical meetings, but the Party would supervise them.

The focus of Party work in the Chinese factory was the same as that of the Soviet postwar methods. The workshop was "the most important unit in the struggle for plan fulfillment and overfulfillment. To run it well is to guarantee the plan."[13] In order to do this, the workshop boss was to use production charts to direct and organize production in their section, to unite the masses by convening regular production conferences and systematizing the section's work, and to organize socialist competitions and encourage emulators and innovators. For this to be successful, the workshop boss must have an intimate knowledge of the shop's technology, closely manage every worker, increase the masses' technical abilities, properly distribute work tasks, hand out rewards and punishments, and assign work according to ability.

The most important work in the workshop, from the CCP's point of view, was agitation and propaganda (*agitprop*) work. This work closely followed the agitators' work, as described in the Soviet management manuals. The Chinese *agitprop* work consisted of five tasks: First, the workshop boss must work to increase the workers' consciousness by teaching them Marxism–Leninism and Mao Zedong thought. Second, he must develop the creativity and warm feelings of the masses toward production. Third, he should strengthen enterprise discipline and production order. Fourth, he should encourage the working masses to study technology so as to be able to fulfill the plan better. And fifth, he must practice economy and protect all state property against saboteurs (*pohuai fenzi*).[14]

The workshop was viewed as a classroom by the *agitprop* department. As one management handbook stated, "We must deeply integrate the political situation, the work tasks, and the masses' thoughts. The work site should be taken as lecture hall, the object as teaching material to carry out work."[15] The managers' handbooks contained detailed explanations of *agitprop* work. The manager could read about how to train *agitprop* workers and how to organize small agitation groups (*xiaohui*), agitation circles (*tuan*), and bigger agitation meetings (*hui*). The content of *agitprop*, the books stated, must always follow a specific format. It had to include a "thought aspect," which included both Marxism-Leninism and Mao Zedong thought, as well as CCP and government decrees. It had to be truthful and clear (according to some unstated CCP standard) and be communicated so that the workers could grasp its content. It had to be concrete and specific, so that the workers would see the connection between state interests and the work of their own factory. And it had to contain an element of struggle so that the workers would have the initiative to accomplish the plan goals.

The methods of agitation and propaganda also followed the Soviet example. First, there was to be an oral form, which meant slogans, reports, meetings, and the reading of newspapers. Slogans were considered the enterprise *agitprop* department's most important contribution. The second aspect of *agitprop* was the small-group meeting, at which the agitator would read newspapers to the workers. The department also staged productions and radio broadcasts. The third feature of *agitprop* included all written communications, which ranged from wall newspapers to blackboard messages, "quick bulletins," and posters. Fourth was the use of drawings and pictures, such as photos of the model workers; cartoons (*manhua*), charts, and diagrams. In addition, the Party created exhibits of technology and the factory's products and a "board of honor" for model workers. It also initiated the use of the red flag, red lamp, and red star, to be given out to workers as rewards for good work.

The Party committee was in charge of maintaining unity in the factory among the manager, the Party organization, the labor union, and the youth group. As mentioned earlier, the goal was to unify these organizations "in thought and in action" under the Party's leadership.[16] In the case of the all-important task of plan fulfillment, for instance, this would mean that the CCP was in charge of and responsible for directing a factorywide mass campaign but that the day-to-day contact with the laborers that this necessitated was the responsibility of the Party's assistants, the labor union and the youth group; the Party was their supervisor. The next section explores the labor union's role in strengthening and solidifying the Communist Party's control of the factory.

The Labor Union Works for Party Control

In ensuring total Party control in the enterprise, the labor union's main tasks were fulfillment of the plan and education of the workers.[17] In order to guarantee production increases, and hence plan fulfillment, the labor union relied on various labor motivation techniques, such as organizing production competitions and other campaigns, and "thought reform," which meant educating and organizing workers, and creating a new workers' attitude toward labor and toward observing labor discipline. Labor union members concentrated on teaching the workers to read during the literacy campaign and on preparing them to uphold the rules of the people's government and to carry out government policies. Its task was to teach workers to protect public property; to oppose corruption, waste, and bureaucracy; and to struggle against any "bad elements."

Both tasks of labor motivation and education were to be carried out by administering socialist competitions and emulation campaigns; they also were meant to increase production and foster socialist attitudes. As we noted, the Party originated each competition and campaign and guided the workers to conclude agreements to achieve the campaign goals and thus fulfill the plan. It was then up to the labor union to organize "the battle," as one factory shop challenged the other in the competition.[18]

Between 1949 and 1953, the labor union concentrated on the movement to encourage "model workers" and on Soviet-style Stakhanovite competitions. Model workers were those who worked so efficiently that they "overfulfilled their plan target." News about them began to appear in mid-1950, complete with their biographies and pictures.[19] The headlines shouted, "Salute the Model Workers!" In addition, large, prestigious conferences in Beijing were arranged for model workers from all over the country. Sometimes, even Mao or other high-ranking Party members would meet and congratulate them.[20]

The most famous model workers were usually small-group leaders, whose groups became identified with the leader's name. The best-known model worker in 1950/1951 was Ma Hengchang, a worker in Machinery Factory No. 5 in Shenyang (Liaoning).[21] Soon after he and his small group had issued a challenge to the entire country, a number of books and articles extolling the virtues of Ma Hengchang's approach appeared.[22]

The Ma Hengchang phenomenon was an integral part of the Chinese competition method, and in many ways, Ma was the Chinese Stakhanov. The Soviet Stakhanovite movement had been widely publicized in China,[23] and indeed, the elements of each resembled the other, with the CCP literature on campaigns paralleling the Soviet handbooks and manuals.

Just as the Soviets had extolled the virtues of the campaign method, the Chinese specialists wrote that the Stakhanovite competition was an excellent way to prod the masses to complete and overfulfill the enterprise production plan. It was also, they wrote, the most rational and powerful organizational tool for enterprise management work, because it guaranteed the enterprise's success.[24] They noted that the Soviets had demonstrated that it was a good method for training management cadres and drawing from among the best workers those who could be educated to become managers, assistant managers, and group leaders. It was also regarded as a good way to teach the masses and help them form a new "labor point of view."[25]

The CCP's literature on campaigns, based as it was on the Soviets' postwar literature, contained all five elements of High Stalinism. The first and most important, of course, was to use the campaigns to enhance the role and increase the Party's authority in the factory. For example, in coordinating the campaigns, the CCP promoted the idea of the Party's indispensable role. In the literature, Party members often were given full credit for such movements, even when the labor union's role was substantial.[26] In one factory, for instance, it was said that the Party was responsible for encouraging a certain worker to "muster up the courage" to go beyond his normal output quota. Once he did, the Party used him as a model for the entire factory. In the end, the Party was credited for the success of the factory's model worker program, which, at least on paper, was administered by the labor union.[27]

The campaigns also contained High Stalinist methods of militarization and patriotism. During the "Resist America Aid Korea"[28] campaign in 1950, for example, the workers were taught that their work at the factory was tantamount to fighting imperialism. As one newspaper stated, "In the Northeast, the workers see every increase in output as a blow to American aggression."[29] Clearly, then, the Party taught the workers who the enemy was and why they should work harder. With the help of the labor union, under the supervision of the Party, the workers would come to see that their role of increasing production in campaigns was indeed a "concrete manifestation of patriotism."[30]

The process also educated the workers in using Soviet-style mass methods, another High Stalinist technique. The campaigns forced the new workers to be socialized in industrial discipline, and it encouraged the more experienced workers to discard their old work habits and work culture. Their new education included an introduction to specific Soviet techniques, such as the work of Kovalyev, who had been a Stakhanovite worker in Moscow in the postwar period.

In addition, all Party and labor union officials had to study. Once they had mastered Kovalyev's methods, they took the message to the workers. The labor union officials were to make the workers understand that the Kovalyev experience would improve discipline, which was the only way to build a new China, which in turn was the only way that the workers' lives could be improved. They told the workers that this was how Soviet workers had achieved their happy lifestyle.

Once the workers were organized in a campaign, their participation functioned, as it had in the postwar Soviet Union, as a way of determining new wage rates. Records were kept on production efficiency, quality, waste control, and safety techniques, and the records were adjusted upward after each campaign.[31] In this way, the labor union and the party could point to the achievements of one branch and set the next period's norms at a somewhat higher rate. In all the work aimed at cementing Party control, both the Party and the labor union could rely on their other helper in the factory, the youth group organization.

The Youth Group: The Party's "Reserve Army"

The youth group was called the "workers' mass political organization." It was often referred to as the Party's most dependable assistant (*zhushou*)[32] or, sometimes, as the Party's reserve army (*houbei jun*).[33] The CCP was in charge of training the leaders of the youth movement so that the youth group could assist the factory Party committee. The youth group's work among workers centered on working with the Party to educate workers, especially the young ones, to make sure they fulfilled the plan, and on carrying out health measures.

The youth group's first task was to assist the Party and the labor union in educating all young workers. As the "school of Marxism, Leninism, and Mao thought" the youth group worked to raise workers' political consciousness and to help them form a correct outlook on life (*rensheng shi*). The group also was to carry out "thought reform" work among all young workers.

The youth group's second task entailed increasing production, that is, developing in all young workers a sense of production activity, creativity, and shock work (working above the norm). Youth group members were to energetically participate in and promote socialist competition, make it possible for the young workers to learn from the other workers' greater production experience, help workers exceed the old production norms, work to increase the number of rationalization proposals, and encourage workers to become model workers. The third task demanded that the youth group be concerned with workers' health, that it develop a physical culture movement and cultural recreation movement. It was the job of the youth organization to "pay attention to youth's special characteristics" and to see that all young people correctly handled their day-to-day problems.

For its work in assisting the Party in the factory, the youth group worked on the campaigns alongside the labor union officials. They were active in the production competitions and the Stakhanov-type, patriotic emulation campaigns. As shown in Chapter 5, they also organized "production conferences" among workers.

For its part in factory motivation work, the youth group organized after-hours study groups to teach the workers about culture and technology. It also launched a new movement called "respect the teacher and love the apprentice," to encourage the workers to learn from and respect more advanced workers, and to improve relations between the two. The youth group relied on drama and art to reach the young workers.[34] In most of its work, the postwar Soviet youth group (Komsomol) literature provided the examples of factory life.

Once the mass organizations were created in an enterprise, the CCP had available to it an array of methods and means to teach, motivate, and engage the workers. The workers were kept busy attending meetings, forming study groups, challenging other workers to compete, and answering such challenges, in a frenzy of political and economic activity. As Lieberthal noted in his study of Tianjin, campaigns as a method of mass mobilization create a crisislike situation that moves and touches its participants and therefore galvanizes the people into action.[35] It is this feature of mass mobilization that exercised control over the Chinese population from 1949 to 1953.

The next section demonstrates how the CCP used its factory mass organizations in campaigns to solidify its control among the population. Although the first mass movements focused simply on economic goals, with each successive effort the emphasis became more political. At the same time, as each campaign got under way, the Communist Party took stronger and stronger control of the process and its results, either on its own or through the labor union and youth group organizations.

Mass Campaigns and Movements

The CCP's first large-scale economic emulation campaign was called the New Records Movement (Xin jilu yundong). It began in the northeast, after the Dongbei (Northeast) Ministry of Industry examined its state industry and announced that waste was an overwhelming problem in most factories. The ministry attributed this to an irregular production rhythm and to the cadres' lack of both organizational and management experience. It said that these factors resulted in low labor productivity, an inefficient use of equipment, and the utter depletion of raw and processed materials.

Before the movement actually began in earnest, the ministry decided that it should strengthen the economic cost–accounting system and develop a mass struggle against waste. It was thought that this was the best way to improve industrial management and to motivate the workers, technicians, and employees to perform better on the job.

Two months went by in the struggle against waste, and in September 1949, the Dongbei People's Government decreed that all the Industrial Ministry's factories and mines were to embark on a mass movement to achieve new records. On October 6, 1949, the *Dongbei ribao* [Dongbei daily] printed the ministry's directive on economic cost accounting. One of the four points in the directive was a call for a mass movement to create new records and fight waste. The Central Committee of the Communist Party of Dongbei then issued a similar article, in which it specifically appealed to the factory party organizations and all Party members to persuade workers to study the government's aforementioned article and to lead the workers. The *Dongbei tongxun* [Dongbei dispatch] of October 11 (issue no. 7) also began a special column called "Collections from the New Records Movement" to help propagandize the new mass movement.[36]

This movement took much from Soviet practice, both from the experience of joint Soviet–Chinese administration in Lushun (Port Arthur) and Dalian and from the postwar five-year plan. What the Soviets probably had already learned from this but did not write about in their literature, the Chinese soon discovered: Records were broken and new standards were set, but such activity was highly disruptive to the production process. What was needed was a focus on leadership and on the workers' and managers' responsibilities. By mid-1950, China's industrial press was full of articles calling for the establishment of a system of responsibility.

At the same time as the calls for a system of responsibility were made, the Party's upper reaches charged its ranks with having become too bureaucratic and with using "commandist" methods. In mid-1950, the Party launched a movement to "rectify," or to correct, the situation. In the first year of CCP power, the Party had recruited new members aggressively, because it had been facing a serious lack of qualified Party personnel.[37] This heavy recruiting led to problems that by mid-1950 obliged the Party to reconsider its recruitment policy and reinvestigate all of its members. It wanted to improve discipline, rid itself of undesirables, and improve its members' training and indoctrination. Although this was a limited campaign, it was carried out from top to bottom, as usual.

In the second half of 1950, the campaigns moved into a new phase. Their purpose remained ostensibly economic, but the political intention became more blatant. Externally, there was the Korean War, and internally, there was "evidence" of Guomindang spies, who became the targets of the "Movement to Suppress Counterrevolutionaries." This campaign has been termed the "most violent campaign in the first two decades of Communist rule."[38] It involved "severe class struggle" and mass public trials to denounce "counterrevolutionaries," as well as workers "pouring out their bitterness" by telling the gathered crowds about their own history of exploitation and abuse.[39]

The Communists used this campaign to eliminate remnants of the Guomindang who may have posed a threat to the CCP. Once the former Guomindang members were turned in or turned themselves in, the CCP was ruthless in carrying out its promise for retribution against former enemies.[40] As some have pointed out, even though the hundreds of thousands of people who were publicly executed during this campaign represented only a small portion of the population, nevertheless, the killings "created an atmosphere of fear and an attitude of submissiveness" that affected the population as a whole.[41] It also, of course, reduced the threat of opposition.

The threat of war in October 1950 provided the justification for the harsh manner in which the "Movement to Suppress Counter-revolutionaries" was carried out. The Korean War furnished the perfect opportunity for the Party to strengthen its legitimacy and garner support among the population. It galvanized the population under a feeling of national crisis, one over which the Party had complete control. In fact, the war gave the Party a free hand to apply stricter rules and to exact sacrifices from the people. Patriotism, for the first time, was openly and aggressively exploited, recalling the mass appeals to patriotism in the Soviet postwar recovery.

On October 13, 1950, just two days before the Chinese officially entered the Korean War, a famous labor hero named Chao Kuoyu and his fellow workers at the Mukden Machine Tool Factory issued a challenge to all other Manchurian workers, for an emulation drive that would "strengthen the fatherland, defend world peace, and oppose American aggression." In the industrial management press, it was said that "the workers are meeting the threats of American imperialist aggressors by harnessing their mounting anger to increased production efforts."[42] Contracts were drawn up in many factories and mines between the workers and the labor union. Every worker's job was evaluated in terms of his or her contribution to the war effort, and workers all across China were encouraged to see their jobs as a donation to the war effort.

This became known as the "Resist America, Aid Korea" campaign. Soon after, another well-known Dongbei labor hero made an emotional, patriotic appeal to other workers, on October 25, 1950: "To protect our great Motherland, to strengthen our national defence, to crush the American imperialist aggressors, I call on you, workers of Northeast China, to raise production!"[43] Then, when workers at a steel plant were challenged by the workers at the Taiyuan Cement Plant in Shansi in December 1950, the cement workers replied: "It is your job to turn out more steel, and we shall do our job in cement. We shall compete to strengthen our national defences and check American aggression."[44]

The "Resist America, Aid Korea" movement was the first campaign that the CCP manipulated into a patriotic movement. In January 1951, the *Renmin ribao* defined patriotism for the Chinese people, stating that patriotism meant

to oppose imperialist aggression and feudal oppression, to safeguard the
fruits of the Chinese people's democratic revolution, to support new
democracy, to stand for progress and oppose backwardness, to support
laboring people, to support the alliance of internationalism of laboring
people of China, the USSR, the People's Democracies and the world, and
to strive for a socialist future.[45]

One of the explicit aims of China's "Resist America, Aid Korea" movement, indeed, was to teach the workers patriotism,[46] and many propagandists' handbooks from 1951 centered on patriotism and how to
instill it.[47] One book stated that "everybody could see that their nice
lives were due to the CCP's and Mao's leadership. Therefore, how can
one who loves his country not work hard?"[48]

Just as the CPSU had done in many of its national campaigns,
especially during the postwar period, the Chinese Communist Party
elevated its goals to a national level and made fulfilling one's work
tasks commensurate with supporting the war effort. Any type of lazi-
ness, absenteeism, or poor-quality work, it was implied, could and
would be equated with the worker's lack of patriotism. In this way,
each worker could feel that his or her job was important to the war
effort, no matter how small or remote it was to the war. In making
pledges to increase production and improve quality for the war effort,
the workers' slogan became

"Machines Are Our Weapons, Factories Our Battlefields!"[49]

At the same time that the CCP was urging all workers to increase
production and quality for the war effort, there was a crisis between
the Party and the labor union organization over operational authority in the factory. Much has been written about this,[50] but basically,
the Party accused the labor union of "economism." This was defined
as becoming too absorbed in the economic concerns of the workers
and seeing the role of the union as somehow independent of that of
the Party. As early as 1949, labor union officials began to complain
that the unions were increasingly being overshadowed by the Party
and youth group organizations. As the latter two organizations
increased their strength, the union found that the workers were less
interested in participating in labor union activities.[51]

The ensuing campaigns emphasized the Party's leading role among
workers and the importance of patriotism. During the second half of
1951, the movement revolved around the "Eliminate Waste, Increase
Production" and the "Increase the Strength of 'Resist America, Aid
Korea'" campaigns, which were vividly portrayed in workers' magazines. In one, there was the story of a factory's leading small group,
which felt that the campaign did not pertain to them and hence continued to waste resources. The factory Party committee noticed this

and called a meeting, at which the Party representative told the workers: "Wipe out waste as if you were wiping out the American devils. We absolutely cannot be self-satisfied; we must increase our vigilance." According to the article, the speech was so inspiring that the wasteful small group discovered its errors and immediately corrected them. The Party committee was credited for this success and for subsequently using this example to inspire other factory small groups.[52]

By September 1951, these campaigns had become blatantly political in nature. The Chinese Communists began the "Three-Anti" campaign, which was directed against the three vices of corruption, waste, and bureaucracy. Although not as violent as the "Movement to Suppress Counterrevolutionaries," millions of people were publicly humiliated and frightened in this campaign to consolidate the regime's hold over labor.[53] Mass meetings were held in cities where local bosses continued to wield influence, and the CCP encouraged the workers to turn against their bosses, to denounce them, and to join the Communist-sponsored labor union.

The Three-Anti activities were led by the Communist Party in the factories, through the committees that were set up to guarantee an increase in production and a decrease in waste. The movement became big and rather bureaucratic itself and at times did result in actual decreases in production (such as in January 1952), just as the Soviets had experienced.[54] In January 1952, the movement expanded to include the private sector (not just the state enterprises), and it blended into another campaign known as the "Five-Anti" Campaign.

The five targets in this campaign were bribing, evading taxes, stealing state property, cheating on government contracts, and stealing state economic information. The movement focused on former industrialists and other representatives of the vaguely defined capitalist class. Under the Party's supervision, the workers waged the struggle against the business class.

This campaign, like previous movements, contained the requisite elements of patriotism, the use of mass organizations, class warfare, and mass rallies at which people recalled "past bitterness." As one Shanghai newspaper summed up the Five-Anti Campaign in June 1952, "Though numerous mass movements have been staged in Shanghai before this, not one of them can approach the present one in scope, extensiveness, organization, discipline, influence, and effect."[55]

During this campaign, committees were organized in all major cities in China in January 1952. Propaganda networks were created; the newspapers and radio were used; and people were specially trained to ferret out "cheaters." Teams of propagandists scoured the city to mobilize the people in helping them hang banners and wall newspapers, and loudspeakers were set up in public places. Mass "struggle" meetings were held in various cities against chosen business representatives. Those who witnessed the campaign describe humiliating tactics of psychological terror.[56] One businessman was interrogated in his underwear for three days, others were handcuffed in their offices for days.

The CCP's campaigns of 1949–1953 resemble in many ways those that took place in the Soviet Union's postwar period. In the Soviet case, the Party was struggling to regain its hold on the workers and a recalcitrant population, just as the CCP needed to do in the "post-liberation" period. In importing the Soviet methods, the CCP transferred to China the elements of High Stalinism, which were quickly adapted to the CCP's endless need to control all aspects of production and of life. As in all processes of adaption and emulation, the new Chinese version of Soviet methods reflected the influence of China's needs and requirements, the most important of which was to solidify Communist control.

Conclusion

A major goal of China's planned social transformation was political control, without which, as the CCP saw it, its "dream of a red factory" could not be realized. This high degree of control was achieved by relying on the formation of mass organizations, which were the most important link between the Chinese Communist Party and the Chinese people in the 1949–1953 period. They were critical to aiding the Communist Party in its goals to mobilize, teach, and control the population, all of which it did by administering mass campaigns. The CCP learned that the mass campaign method was probably the easiest way for a country poor in resources to mobilize its population toward a common goal. This was so because such campaigns "shunted aside routine procedure and legal niceties to focus on the most pressing problem of the day."[57] They were effective at strengthening Party control but just as the Soviets found, were not economically efficient or particularly productive. In fact, they severely disrupted the production process.

The mass campaigns provided excellent training in the ways of socialist behavior, actions, and thought. The use of mass organizations in a campaign also worked against any anti-communist opposition, since the mass organizations were stronger, were organized nationally (as opposed to regionally), and were simply bigger. Eventually, millions of people came to belong to and be influenced by some sort of mass organization.

As the Soviet model was being studied and its emulation was being encouraged all around China, the CCP kept launching mass movements and campaigns. The particular blend of an extremely political, controlling, and intrusive management model with the CCP's need for total control resulted in massive political repression and terror.[58] In the process of politicizing the workers, the CCP took militarization a step further, by introducing the concepts of "class" and "class struggle," thus immediately delineating class lines. As Lynn White illustrated in his work, even in the early years when former capitalists managed the economic organizations for the Communists, they were already marked and labeled "capitalists," as opposed to the "proletariat." This laid the groundwork for future "struggles" against any "bad elements" that the Party could discover.

One of the consequences of studying the Soviet Union's postwar period was that the CCP emulated a model characterizing a period of extreme political control. In no other period of Soviet history did the leader and the Communist Party have such boundless power and authority as Stalin had in the postwar period. The management model that the CCP adopted in the early 1950s was a product of this period, and the Chinese outcome indeed was an offspring of High Stalinism. By concentrating on this period of Soviet history, the CCP adopted the features of an excessive model as a starting point in the PRC's development.

The postwar model introduced the High Stalinist elements of fear, intimidation, and even terror into mass politics. Because of its need for political control, the example of the Soviet model, which the Chinese press presented as legitimate, allowed the CCP to rationalize and justify its reliance on these methods. As we saw, the level of coercion increased and the level of class lines deepened with each successive mass campaign, as the CCP strengthened its hold on the population.

7

The Triumph of High Stalinism

At the beginning of this book, a question was raised about the enduring strength, power, and authority of Chinese communism. To answer this, it was necessary to take a close look at the origins of Chinese communist institutions. It was found that the structure and form of Chinese communist power was rooted in the CCP's impressions of how the Soviet model functioned during Stalin's most excessive last years, the years of High Stalinism.

The CCP relied on a vast array of Soviet books from this period, most of which the Chinese themselves translated from Russian. I argue that the CCP did this to answer its urgent, domestic requirements in the face of insubstantial Soviet help during the early years. In this book, I examined the literature that the CCP translated in the field of industrial management and organization, as the Chinese Communists pursued their "dream" of an industrialized and modernized China.

The question was asked as to why the Chinese communists had chosen in particular the High Stalinist model of 1946–1950. Although this issue is never addressed in either the Soviet or Chinese sources, I speculate that there may have been several considerations. It might be that the CCP saw the Soviet postwar recovery as a good model for China's reconstruction after years of upheaval and war. It might also be that Mao himself coveted Stalin's supreme position in the USSR and wanted a similar role as indisputable ruler of China. Or it could simply be that the Chinese communists did not feel it worthwhile to work through the Soviet history of collectivization and industrialization because they assumed that they would find a Chinese solution to these problems. Finally, it is possible that the CCP saw that the High Stalinist period, with its aura of Communist Party invincibility, would provide the best methods for solidifying its own power in China.

The relationship between China and the Soviet Union was not a close one, nor did it improve much once Mao and Stalin met in December 1949. Even after the Soviets formally recognized the PRC in October 1949, substantial Soviet aid did not arrive until after Stalin's death in 1953. Until then, the CCP relied mostly on its own translation of written materials and, of course, the books that the Soviets chose to translate into Chinese, as seen in Chapter 1. During the 1949–1953 period, most Chinese editors and translators who were issuing handbooks that were to teach the Soviet methods to Chinese laborers admitted that they had had little experience. In one Chinese worker's political textbook, the preface states that not only was the volume produced very quickly but also none of the editors had had any experience in the workers' movement (*meiyou gongren yundongde jingyan*).[1] Nor had very many of them actually lived in the system about which they were writing.

The Worst of Stalinism in Translation

The Chinese version of the Soviet industrial enterprise management model, which was described in Chapter 3, was based on the CCP's reading of the written sources and reflected its own needs and interests as well. Since the translated books and articles were almost universally from the Soviet postwar period, they all emphasized the significant role of the Communist Party's power and control in industrial management. In fact, we discovered in the accounts of Party management in enterprises, the system was little more than thinly veiled coercion and intimidation used to force people to comply with Party demands. The aura of fear was pervasive.

Stalin himself commanded a fearful respect among the people and even (one might say, especially) among his closest associates.[2] For instance, N. Fedorenko, who accompanied Mao Zedong to Moscow in December 1949 and worked as his interpreter for Stalin, vividly described the fear and anxiety that Stalin caused among those around him. Fedorenko describes his own fright when, as he was trying to understand what Mao had said in his regional Chinese dialect so as to render it correctly in Russian, Stalin "imperiously" demanded: "Is this conspiring going to go on much longer?" During the postwar years, when fear and respect for Stalin were at their height, even the lowliest Party functionary at a factory could (and, according to the literature, did) use this fear to extract compliance among the work force.

In pursuit of its goal of socialist industrialization, the CCP translated detailed accounts about the structure of factory administration and about the role of the factory Party committee, the labor union, and the youth group. As we noted, every Soviet account illustrated how the Party both took charge of the plan's fulfillment and directed the efforts of the factory labor union and youth group to realize this goal. The lessons of this model, especially in the idealized form that the Chinese studied, coincided very nicely with the CCP's primary goal of political control.

Political Control over Economic Rationality

Because the CCP decided to study the Soviet Fourth Five-Year Plan of 1946–1950, it was necessary to take a new look at the Soviet postwar period, in particular, to understand industrial management and organization. In so doing, several important aspects emerged. First, the postwar plan fulfillment methods were so unworkable and economically counterproductive that the plan was secretly abandoned halfway through the five-year period. Second, five particular elements— the five precepts of High Stalinism—were found to characterize the management practices of the period.

The management model that the CCP emulated in the early 1950s reflected more the elements of High Stalinism than of socialism, and this, more than anything else, meant a role for a supreme, unquestionable leader and his indisputable Party. In the factory, it meant CCP rule that relied on Party authority and coercion in all affairs. High Stalinism as a management system featured intense Communist Party involvement in the day-to-day operation of enterprises; the pervasive militarization of industrial management; heavy reliance on "mass" methods, emphasis on the education of all workers in Marxism-Leninism to inculcate in them the proper worldview, and the linking of economic goals with Soviet patriotism. All five of these features appeared later in some form in the adapted Chinese management model.

The first feature of this model was the Communist Party's intrusive methods of worker control in Soviet factories to push workers toward plan fulfillment. The second feature of this model was the use of "mass" methods, such as campaigns, which were displayed in great detail in the Soviet management handbooks. With massive Party supervision, the mass methods were said to accomplish large goals with little money. The third feature, which was no doubt a manifestation of the militarization that Soviet society underwent during World War II, was the pervasive use of military terms in the management literature. The fourth feature of the Soviet model of this period was the Stalinist belief that the workers could be educated and changed. The Communist Party's programs concentrated on teaching workers the tenets of

Marxism-Leninism, on "shaping" their attitude toward work, and on "improving" their political consciousness. The last feature of the Soviet model of 1946–1950 was the linking of economic goals with patriotism. The workers were told that each of their tasks was vital to the development of socialism, that every job in the enterprise was linked with national goals.

High Stalinism was a system that mandated a great deal of Communist Party participation in management, often in an intrusive and coercive manner. By Stalin's own decree, the Party was responsible for the workers' fulfilling their plan norms, and in response, the Party became very active in managing the workers' time, in mobilizing them to participate in socialist competitions, and in forcing them to fulfill and overfulfill the norms. The effect of stressing political over economic management, the emphasis on Stakhanovite competitions that disrupted the normal routine of production, and the great number of political meetings with Communist Party "agitators" during and after the workday all finally took their toll at the end of 1947, when the plan was secretly dropped. But this was probably not known to the CCP, and if it had been, it no doubt would not have mattered.

CCP Goals: Three Explicit, One Implicit

The Chinese Communist Party's emphasis on its political agenda can be clearly seen in the processes of adapting institutions and in the organizational forms that were created in response to the CCP's three goals in 1949. The goals were to establish the means for carrying out socialist industrialization, worker socialization, and control. The previous chapters described the CCP's three goals and how the Party advocated, on the basis of Soviet writings, their attainment. The leitmotif of all Chinese Communist writings of this period, like the Soviet postwar literature, was the justification of Communist Party control and power in the enterprise. This was the CCP's implicit goal.

Socialist Industrialization

The CCP's first problem in carrying out socialist industrialization was to recruit and train laborers. In many ways, China's labor problems were similar to those in postwar Soviet Union. Both China and the postwar USSR suffered from gross shortages of qualified industrial laborers, which is why the Chinese studied Gosplan USSR's postwar recruitment and training programs. But China's more serious problem was its lack of highly skilled industrial workers, which is why the Soviets' factory training programs and technical schools (which, according to Soviet accounts, produced the needed laborers) were of interest to the Chinese. Finally, the Chinese communists wanted to attain stricter control of its workers, a problem that was solved in Stalin's

USSR by relying on the factory Communist Party organization and its subsidiaries, the labor union and youth group in industrial enterprises. The CCP appeared to believe that the CPSU's postwar methods were responsible for encouraging a very war-weary population to undertake the massive effort of economic recovery. For this reason alone the model was worth emulating.

The CCP adopted Soviet management principles to create its own "Industrial Management Mechanism," as seen in Chapter 4. Not only did the CCP adopt the Soviet precepts, but it also made additions that further strengthened the Party's role in the enterprise. Of the six adopted Soviet precepts, four of them concerned Party responsibility for management: the primacy of the Party and Marxism-Leninism, the Party's "right of control," one-man management, and democratic centralism. To this basic model, the Chinese added the two more Party-related elements of socialist competition and a Bolshevik style of management.

Because of the need for CCP power and authority in the factory, the Chinese also adapted the imported management model to include additional elements, in a program called "Democracy of Management." This called for the formation of factory management committees (which were administered by the factory director and other administration personnel, the labor union chief, and other workers' representatives), a factory management committee standing committee (composed of the factory director, the Party head, and the labor union chief), and the factory employees' and workers' conference (directed by the labor union). In practice, as the Chinese themselves wrote, the purpose of these organizations was to ensure that the factory administration, Party, and union bodies acted as one, under the leadership of the most powerful body, the Communist Party.

This mixture of an adapted Soviet management model with the various committees in the factory was unwieldy in practice. It did, however, answer the CCP's need for political control, thus making the CCP's political agenda the most significant influence on the adaptation of Soviet management structures and methods. The only enduring and consistent element in all of the management programs in the 1949–1953 period was the power of the Communist Party in the enterprise.

Socialization

The CCP's program for worker socialization between 1949 and 1953 is the second example of the fusing of Soviet and Chinese ideas with the aim of CCP control. One important reason for altering and augmenting the Soviet model was China's lack of an industrial working class. As explained in Chapter 5, the CCP approach was twofold: It produced workers' handbooks to teach the new socialist worldview to the newly created Chinese proletariat, and it restructured factory relations on the basis of what it knew about Soviet factory administration.

The workers' handbooks reflected the CCP's grounding in the Soviet idealized literature; in fact, a positive image of Soviet society was used to justify the CCP's rule. The handbooks presented an entire belief system to the Chinese workers. They were designed to discredit the "bad, old China" by recounting a history of worker exploitation and illuminating the misery and poverty of life before the communists took power. The workers were taught about class struggle and class hatred and were soon labeled and divided into classes. All of this was to convince the workers that their lives had been wretched before CCP "liberation" and that under communist rule, their lives would be happy and easy.

To augment these new teachings, the CCP also created a socialist factory structure, since the Chinese believed (on the basis of their reading of Soviet literature) that for the purposes of socialization, nothing was more important than the creation of mass organizations (the Party, labor union, and youth group). The management texts made it clear that the Party would direct the other two organizations in the factory.

From the tasks set forth for the mass organizations in the Chinese factory, it was apparent that socialization meant informing the workers of the Party's resolutions (which was called "raising their consciousness"); it meant Party supervision of the workers' political, economic, and cultural development; it meant recruiting new members into the Party; and it entailed "thought reform" by the Party among the workers. "Thought problems" were to be solved by immersing the worker in Marxist–Leninist–Maoist teachings.

To teach the workers its lessons, the CCP followed the Soviet practice of organizing mass campaigns, so as to "keep the leading role of the Party in the minds of the workers at all times." The mandate of the labor union and youth group was the same: to assist the Party in socializing the workers and in creating a new labor attitude among workers. Thus the point of socialization was not simply to create a proletariat that would produce well but also to convince the new working class of the CCP's legitimacy in society and of primacy in industrial management.

Worker Control

The third example of the influence of the CCP's political agenda on the adaptation of Soviet institutions was its programs to regulate and control the workers. In 1949 the CCP was faced with what could be either an asset or a disadvantage: a very large population. The CCP wanted to institute control over this population; so following the example of the Soviet Union, it mandated the establishment of mass organizations in all enterprises. These organizations quickly became the most important link between the Chinese Communist Party and the masses. They were indispensable in assisting the Communist Party in its goals to mobilize, teach, and control the population.

Once the organizations were formed, they were able to draw millions of people into Party-administered mass campaigns. These campaigns began simply as a method to accomplish economic goals (i.e., to stop waste and to increase production) but quickly evolved into campaigns with large political aims. Again, by studying the post-war Stalinist example, the Chinese learned about equating economic performance with patriotism or about making an economic campaign into a "battle," but because of the CCP's main agenda of political control, the campaigns evolved into vehicles for regulating and manipulating the population.

Although the CCP naturally drew on its own previous experience with mass politics, its main source of information on techniques was a written literature that was infused with the High Stalinist elements of the Soviet postwar period. The Soviet model introduced the Stalinist elements of fear, intimidation, and even terror into mass politics. Because of its need for political control, the example of the Soviet model (made to look legitimate by the Chinese press) allowed the CCP to rationalize and justify its reliance on these methods.

The Lasting Lessons of High Stalinism

This book has argued that the early structures and lessons that the CCP took from High Stalinism created a powerful and authoritative Communist Party in China from its earliest time in power. The CCP's agenda of political control mixed with a model characterized by High Stalinist elements had several consequences for China's development. First, the Chinese environment became politicized to a greater degree and more quickly than it otherwise might have been. Second, the Chinese Communist Party probably wielded more power in society and in industrial management than did its Soviet counterpart. Third, the level of CCP intrusion and coercion in management, based on what it thought had worked in the Soviet model, was quite high very early in the history of the PRC. Fourth, as a result both of the CCP's dominance of all political relations and of its power, class lines were drawn more deeply and earlier, thus setting the stage for future class struggles. This was certainly seen in the succession of mass movements and campaigns over the 1949–1953 period.[3]

The purpose of this book is not to take away from the CCP's successes in China. Indeed, the CCP did fulfill its "dream of a red factory." It created a Chinese working class that was conversant with Stalinist and Maoist language and actions; it replaced the old gang-boss system with a new one; and it worked to improve the lives of millions of workers and employees. But its reliance on such a bleak stage of Soviet history, mixed with its own political needs, added a needless, coercive, and menacing aspect to its power. And that aspect is the most enduring, as the world saw at Tiananmen Square in 1989.

Appendix: The Soviet Union and China Sign Agreements in Moscow, February 14, 1950

Negotiations were recently held in Moscow between Joseph V. Stalin, chairman of the Council of Ministers of the USSR, and A. Y. Vyshinsky, minister of Foreign Affairs of the USSR, on the one hand, and Mao Zedong, chairman of the People's Republic of China and Zhou Enlai, prime minister of the State Administrative Council and minister of Foreign Affairs, on the other, during which important political and economic questions on relations between the Soviet Union and the People's Republic of China were considered.

These negotiations, which proceeded in an atmosphere of cordiality and friendly mutual understanding, confirmed the desire of both parties to strengthen and develop in every way relations of friendship and cooperation between them, and their desire to cooperate for the purpose of ensuring universal peace and the security of the nations.

The negotiations ended in the signing in the Kremlin on February 14 of the following:

1. A Treaty of Friendship, Alliance, and Mutual Assistance Between the Soviet Union and the People's Republic of China.
2. An agreement on the Chinese Changchun Railway, Port Arthur, and Dalny, in accordance with which, after signing a peace treaty with Japan, the Chinese Changchun Railway would be handed over to the complete ownership of the People's Republic of China, and Soviet troops would be withdrawn from Port Arthur.

3. An agreement on the granting by the government of the Soviet Union to the government of the People's Republic of China of long-term economic credits to pay for deliveries of industrial and railway equipment from the USSR.

The aforementioned treaty and agreements were signed on behalf of the USSR by A. Y. Vyshinsky and on behalf of the People's Republic of China by Zhou Enlai.

In connection with the signing of the Treaty of Friendship, Alliance, and Mutual Assistance and the agreement on the Chinese Changchun Railway, Port Arthur, and Dalny, Zhou Enlai and Vyshinsky exchanged notes to the effect that the respective treaty and agreements concluded on August 14, 1945, between China and the Soviet Union had become invalid and also that both governments affirmed a full guarantee of the independent position of the Mongolian People's Republic as a result of the referendum of 1945 and of the establishment with it of diplomatic relations by the People's Republic of China.

Simultaneously, Zhou Enlai and Vyshinsky also exchanged notes on the decision of the Soviet government to hand over gratis to the government of the People's Republic of China that property acquired by Soviet economic organizations from Japanese owners in Manchuria and also on the decision of the Soviet government to hand over gratis to the government of the People's Republic of China all buildings of the former military cantonment in Peking.

The full texts of the aforementioned treaty and agreements are as follows:

Treaty of Friendship, Alliance, and Mutual Assistance Between the Union of Soviet Socialist Republics and the People's Republic of China

The Presidium of the Supreme Soviet of the Union of Soviet Socialist Republics and the Central People's Government of the People's Republic of China;

Filled with determination jointly to prevent, by the consolidation of friendship and cooperation between the Union of Soviet Socialist Republics and the People's Republic of China, the rebirth of Japanese imperialism and a repetition of aggression on the part of Japan or any other state that should unite in any for with Japan in acts of aggression.

Imbued with the desire to consolidate lasting peace and universal security in the Far East and throughout the world in conformity with the aims and principles of the United Nations organization;

Profoundly convinced that the consolidation of good neighborly relations and friendship between the Union of Soviet Socialist Republics and the People's Republic of China meets the fundamental interests of the peoples of the Soviet Union and China;

Resolved for this purpose to conclude the present treaty and appointed as their plenipotentiary representatives:

The Presidium of the Supreme Soviet of the Union of Soviet Socialist Republics—Andrei Yanuaryevich Vyshinsky, Minister of Foreign Affairs of the Union of Soviet Socialist Republics;

The Central People's Government of the People's Republic of China—Zhou Enlai, Prime Minister of the State Administrative Council and Minister of Foreign Affairs of China;

Who, after exchange of their credentials, found in due form and good order, agreed on the following:

Article I

Both High Contracting Parties undertake jointly to take all the necessary measures at their disposal for the purpose of preventing a repetition of aggression and violation of peace on the part of Japan or any other state that should unite with Japan, directly or indirectly, in acts of aggression. In the event of the High Contracting Parties' being attacked by Japan or states allied with it, and thus being involved in a state of war, the other High Contracting Party will immediately render military and other assistance with all the means at its disposal.

The High Contracting Parties also declare their readiness in the spirit of sincere cooperation to participate in all international actions aimed at ensuring peace and security throughout the world and will do all in their power to achieve the speediest implementation of these tasks.

Article II

Both the High Contracting Parties undertake by means of mutual agreement to strive for the earliest conclusion of a peace treaty with Japan, jointly with the other Powers that were allies during the Second World War.

Article III

Both High Contracting Parties undertake not to conclude any alliance directed against the other High Contracting Party and not to take part in any coalition or in actions or measures directed against the other High Contracting Party.

Article IV

Both High Contracting Parties will consult each other in regard to all important international problems affecting the common interests of the Soviet Union and China, being guided by the interests of the consolidation of peace and universal security.

Article V

Both the High Contracting Parties undertake, in the spirit of friendship and cooperation and in conformity with the principles of equality, mutual interests, and also mutual respect for the state sovereignty and territorial integrity and noninterference in internal affairs of the other High Contracting Party, to develop and consolidate economic and cultural ties between the Soviet Union and China, to render to each other every possible economic assistance, and to carry out the necessary economic cooperation.

Article VI

The present treaty comes into force immediately upon its ratification; the exchange of instruments of ratification will take place in Peking.

The present treaty will be valid for thirty years. If neither High Contracting Parties gives notice one year before the expiration of this term of its desire to denounce the treaty, it shall remain in force for another five years and will be extended in compliance with this rule.

Done in Moscow on February 14, 1950, in two copies, each in the Russian and Chinese languages, both texts having equal force.

Agreement Between the Union of Soviet Socialist Republics and the People's Republic of China on the Chinese Changchun Railway, Port Arthur, and Dalny

The Presidium of the Supreme Soviet of the Union of Soviet Socialist Republics and the Central People's Government of the People's Republic of China state that since 1945 radical changes have occurred in the situation in the Far East, namely, Imperialist Japan suffered defeat; the reactionary Guomindang government was overthrown; China has become a People's Democratic Republic; and in China a new, people's government was formed that has united the whole of China, carried out a policy of friendship and cooperation with the Soviet Union, and proved its ability to defend the state independence and territorial integrity of China and the national honor and dignity of the Chinese people.

The Presidium of the Supreme Soviet of the Union of Soviet Socialist Republics and the Central People's Government of the People's Republic of China maintain that this new situation permits a new approach to the question of the Chinese Changchun Railway, Port Arthur, and Dalny.

In conformity with these new circumstances, the Presidium of the Supreme Soviet of the Union of Soviet Socialist Republics and the Central People's Government of the People's Republic of China have decided to conclude the present agreement on the Chinese Changchun Railway, Port Arthur, and Dalny.

Article I

Both High Contracting Parties have agreed that the Soviet Government will transfer gratis to the government of the People's Republic of China all its rights in the joint administration of the Chinese Changchun Railway, with all the property belonging to the railway. The transfer will be effected immediately upon the conclusion of a peace treaty with Japan, but not later than the end of 1952.

Pending a transfer, the now existing position of the Soviet–Chinese joint administration of the Chinese Changchun Railway remains unchanged; however, the order of filling posts by representatives of the Soviet and Chinese sides, upon the coming into force of the present agreement, will be changed, and there will be established an alternating filling of posts for a definite period of time (director of the railway, chairman of the Central Board, and others).

In regard to concrete methods of effecting the transfer, they will be agreed on and determined by the governments of both High Contracting Parties.

Article II

Both High Contracting Parties have agreed that Soviet troops will be withdrawn from the jointly utilized naval base of Port Arthur and that the installations in this area will be handed over to the government of the People's Republic of China immediately upon the conclusion of a peace treaty with Japan, but not later than the end of 1952, with the government of the PRC compensating the Soviet Union for expenses incurred in the restoration and construction of installations effected by the Soviet Union since 1945.

For the period pending the withdrawal of Soviet troops and the transfer of the above installations, the governments of the Soviet Union and China will appoint an equal number of military representatives for organizing a joint Chinese–Soviet Military Commission that will be in charge of military affairs in the area of Port Arthur; concrete measures in this sphere will be determined by the joint Chinese–Soviet Military Commission within three months upon the coming into force of the present agreement and shall be implemented upon the approval of these measures by the governments of both countries.

The civil administration in the aforementioned area shall be in the direct charge of the government of the People's Republic of China. Pending the withdrawal of Soviet troops, the zone of billeting of Soviet troops in the area of Port Arthur will remain unaltered in conformity with the now existing frontiers.

In the event of either of the High Contracting Parties being subjected to aggression on the part of Japan or any state that should unite with Japan and, as a result of this, being involved in military operations, China and the Soviet Union, may, on the proposal of the government of the People's Republic of China and with the agreement of the Soviet government, jointly use the naval base of Port Arthur in the interests of conducting joint military operations against the aggressor.

Article III

Both High Contracting Parties have agreed that the question of Port Dalny must be further considered upon the conclusion of a peace treaty with Japan.

In regard to the administration in Dalny, it fully belongs to the government of the People's Republic of China.

All property now existing in Dalny provisionally in charge of or under lease to the Soviet side is to be taken over by the government of the People's Republic of China. For carrying out work involved in the receipt of the aforementioned property, the governments of the Soviet Union and China will appoint three representatives from each side for organizing a joint commission that in the course of three months after the coming into force of the present agreement shall determine the concrete methods of transfer of property and, after approval of the proposals of the Joint Commission by the governments of both countries, will complete their implementation in the course of 1950.

Article IV

The present agreement comes into force on the day of its ratification. The exchange of instruments of ratification will take place in Peking.

Done in Moscow on February 14, 1950, in two copies, each in the Russian and Chinese languages, both texts having equal force.

Agreement Between the Union of Soviet Socialist Republics and the People's Republic of China on Granting Credits to the People's Republic of China

In connection with the consent of the Government of the Union of Soviet Socialist Republics to grant the request of the Central People's Government of the People's Republic of China on giving China credits for paying for equipment and other materials that the Soviet Union has agreed to deliver to China, both governments have agreed on the following:

Article I

The Government of the Union of Soviet Socialist Republics grants the Central People's Government of the People's Republic of China credits, calculated in dollars, amounting to 300 million American dollars, taking thirty-five American dollars to one ounce of fine gold.

In view of the extreme devastation of China as a result of prolonged hostilities on its territory, the Soviet government has agreed to grant credits on favorable terms of 1 percent annual interest.

Article II

The credits mentioned in Article I will be granted in the course of five years, as from January 1, 1950, in equal portions of one-fifth of the credits in the course of each year, for payments for deliveries from the USSR of equipment and materials, including equipment for electric power stations, metallurgical and engineering plants; equipment for mines for the production of coal and ores; railway and other transport equipment; and rails and other material for the restoration and development of the national economy of China.

The assortment, quantities, prices, and dates of deliveries of equipment and materials will be determined under a special agreement of the parties; prices will be determined on the basis of prices obtaining of the world markets.

Any credits that remain unused in the course of one annual period may be used in subsequent annual periods.

Article III

The Central People's Government of the People's Republic of China repays the credits mentioned in Article I, as well as interest on them, with deliveries of raw materials, tea, gold, and American dollars. Prices for raw materials and tea and quantities and dates of deliveries will be determined on the basis of prices obtaining on the world markets.

Repayment of credits is effected in the course of ten years in equal annual parts—one-tenth yearly of the sum total of received credits not later than December 31, 1954, and the last on December 31, 1963.

Payment of interest on credits, calculated from the day of drawing the respective fraction of the credits, is effected every six months.

Article IV

For clearance with regard to the credits envisaged by the present agreement the Statement Bank of the USSR and National Bank of the People's Republic of China shall open special accounts and jointly establish the order of clearance and accounting under the present agreement.

Article V

The present agreement comes into force on the day of its signing and is subject to ratification. The exchange of instruments of ratification will take place in Peking.

Done in Moscow on February 14, 1950, in two copies, each in the Russian and Chinese languages, both texts having equal force.

Signed:

By the Authorization of the Presidium of the Supreme Soviet of the Union of Soviet Socialist Republics, A. Y. Vyshinsky;

By the Authorization of the Central People's Government of the People's Republic of China, Zhou Enlai.

Notes

Chapter 1

1. This book focuses on the roots of communist political power and authority, which should not be confused with the origins of Chinese communism. An excellent book on the latter topic is that by Arlif Dirlik, *The Origins of Chinese Communism* (New York: Oxford University Press, 1989).

2. For a good description of the Yenan years, see Mark Selden, *The Yenan Way in Revolutionary China* (Cambridge, MA: Harvard University Press, 1971).

3. Mao Tse-tung, *Selected Works of Mao Tse-tung* (Peking: Foreign Languages Press, 1977), vol. 5, p. 17.

4. See the Appendix for a complete text of the agreement.

5. The best introduction to the early 1950s is by Frederick C. Teiwes, "Establishment and Consolidation of the New Regime, in *The People's Republic, Part I*, ed. Roderick MacFarquhar and John K. Fairbank, vol. 14 of *The Cambridge History of China* (Cambridge: Cambridge University Press), pp. 51–143. Also see Teiwes's excellent book on Gao Gang, *Politics at Mao's Court* (Armonk, NY: M. E. Sharpe, 1990), esp. chap. 1.

6. Nai-Ruenn Chen and Walter Galenson define the Soviet model that China allegedly copied as one that began in 1928. See their *The Chinese Economy Under Communism* (Chicago: Aldine, 1969), p. 33. Andrew Walder refers to the 1930s model of Soviet industrialization in *Communist Neo-Traditionalism, Work and Authority in Chinese Industry* (Berkeley and Los Angeles: University of California Press, 1986), pp. 114–22. Jan S. Prybyla, in *The Political Economy of Communist China* (Scranton, PA: International Textbook, 1970), uses the Soviet late 1920s and early 1930s, as does K. C. Yeh, "Soviet and Communist China Industrialization Strategies," in *Soviet and Chinese Commu-*

nism: Similarities and Differences, ed. Donald W. Treadgold (Seattle: University of Washington Press, 1967). In his massive work, *Industrial Society in Communist China* (Cambridge: Cambridge University Press, 1977), Barry Richman also neglects to define precisely the period of the Soviet model to which he refers.

7. Martin K. Whyte, "Bureaucracy and Modernization in China: The Maoist Critique," *American Sociological Review* 38 (April 1973): 149–63.

8. These criticisms can be found in Mao Tse-tung, *A Critique of Soviet Economics,* trans. Moss Roberts (New York: Monthly Review Press, 1977).

9. See Stephen Andors, *China's Industrial Revolution: Politics, Planning and Management* (New York: Pantheon, 1977); Charles Hoffmann, *The Chinese Worker* (Albany: State University of New York Press, 1974); and William Brugger. *Democracy and Organisation in the Chinese Industrial Enterprise* (Cambridge: Cambridge University Press, 1976), who refers sometimes to the Soviet model of the late 1940s but in general assumes that it meant strict line-authority and one-man management.

10. Andrew Walder, "Some Ironies of the Maoist Legacy in Industry," in *The Transition to Socialism in China,* ed. Mark Selden and Victor Lippit (Armonk, NY: M. E. Sharpe, 1982), pp. 215–37.

11. It is not possible to assert with any degree of certainty that Stalin, or even Mao for that matter, actually believed that one must conform in thought as well as in action.

12. For an interesting discussion of political and ideological struggles in China, including a more standard definition of Maoism, see Dorothy A. Solinger, ed., *Three Visions of Chinese Socialism* (Boulder, CO: Westview Press, 1984).

13. *Zhongguo zong shumu* [Chinese general title catalogue] (Beijing: Xinhua shudian biandian, 1955).

14. These included, for example, D. Goginava, *Partiinii kontrol' na predpriyatii* [Party control in the enterprise] (Moscow: Gospolitizdat, 1949); O. Kremnyeva, *Opyt politicheskoi agitatsii na predpriyatii* [The experience of political agitation in the enterprise] (Moscow: Gospolitizdat, 1948); G. M. Malenkov, *O zadachakh partiinykh organizatsii v oblasti promyshlennosti i transporta* [On the tasks of party organizations in the areas of industry and transport] (Moscow: Gospolitizdat, 1941); P. Mogilenko and V. Zasetskii. *Organizatsiya raboty proizvodsvennykh soveshchanii* [Organizational work of the production conference] (Moscow: Profizdat, 1950); V. Murachev and M. Koshonina, *Naglyadnaya agitatsiya na predpriyatii* [Visual agitation at the enterprise] (Moscow: Gospolitizdat, 1953); A. F. Rumyantsev, *Organizatsiya upravleniya promyshlennost'yu SSSR* [The organization of industrial management in the USSR] (Moscow: Vyshaya partiinaya shkola pri TsK KPSS, 1953); V. N. Shchepanskii, *Massogo-politicheskaya rabota na zavode* [Mass-political work at the factory] (Moscow: Gospolitizdat, 1949); A. Zhuravlev, *Agitator—organizator sotsialisticheskogo sorevnovaniya* [The agitator is the organizer of socialist competition] (Moscow: Gospolitizdat, 1948).

15. Chinese scholars often point to the important influence of Soviet publications on China's scholarship and thinking. See the discussion of the importance of Stalin's *Concise Course in the History of the CPSU (Bolsheviks)* on the development of the CCP, in Li Mingsan, "Important Topics Promotive of

the Study of the History of the CCP," *Qiushi* 11 (1988): 43–44, trans. Foreign Broadcast Information Service, February 3, 1989, pp. 16–18.

16. Robert C. Tucker, "Stalinism as Revolution from Above," in *Stalinism; Essays in Historical Interpretation*, ed. Robert C. Tucker (New York: Norton, 1977), pp. 106–8.

17. Bai Yuan and Bai Shi, eds., "Problems of Party–Masses Relationship in the Enterprise," *Xuexi Sulian qiye gongzuo jingyan* [We study the experience of Soviet enterprise work] (Beijing: Dazhong shudian, 1950), vol. 3.

18. Seweryn Bialer includes this period in his excellent chapter on "mature Stalinism," which spans the larger time period of 1938 to 1953. See Seweryn Bialer, *Stalin's Successors; Leadership, Stability, and Change in the Soviet Union* (Cambridge: Cambridge University Press, 1980). Also see William G. Rosenberg and Marilyn B. Young, *Transforming Russia and China; Revolutionary Struggle in the Twentieth Century* (New York: Oxford University Press, 1982).

19. Dmitri Volkogonov, *Stalin: Triumph and Tragedy*, ed. and trans. Harold Shukman (London: Weidenfeld and Nicolson, 1991), p. 502.

20. There were hints as early as 1941 that the CPSU was calling an inordinate number of meetings at work. In a pamphlet on the tasks of the party organizations in industry and transport, G. M. Malenkov wrote that the great number of meetings in the factory was a serious problem. In the pamphlet, he absolutely forbade workers to be called to meetings, sent on campaigns of any sort, or required to serve on committees during the workday. See G. M. Malenkov, *O zadachakh partiinykh organizatsii v oblasti promyshlennosti i transporta* [On the tasks of party organizations in industry in transport] (Moscow: Gosudarstvennoe izdatel'stvo politicheskoi literatury, 1949).

21. Soviet China specialists have noted the "militaristic character" of Chinese industrial management, but they have attributed it wholly to the "special role played by the PLA" during the civil war and the revolution. See V. N. Remyga, *Sistema upravleniya promyshlennost'yu KNR (1949–1975)* [The industrial management system of the PRC (1949–1975)], diss. abstract (Moscow: Institute of the Far East, 1977), p. 7.

22. Military terminology in political and economic affairs is an established Soviet tradition, beginning with Lenin (see Volkogonov, *Stalin: Triumph and Tragedy*, p. 168). Stalin continued this tradition throughout his reign, beginning with the First Five-Year Plan of 1928. See the description in Robert C. Tucker, *Stalin in Power: The Revolution from Above, 1928–1941* (New York: Norton, 1990), pp. 93–94.

23. One cannot help but think of the old Soviet criticism of Mao that he early on began to encourage his own cult of personality. The Soviets cite, for instance, the 2.4 million copies of Mao's works that were published by October 1951 and the officially mandated six to fifteen hours a week devoted to studying his "thought" at universities and state institutions in that same year. The numbers can be found in *Narodnii Kitai* [People's China] 4 (1951): 28, and were quoted by O. B. Borisov and B. T. Koloskov, *Sovetsko–Kitaiskie otnosheniya, 1945–1977* [Soviet–Chinese relations, 1945–1977] (Moscow: Mysl', 1977), pp. 135–36.

24. I owe this particular method, which is crucial to the argument, to the work of Gilbert Rozman, in his *A Mirror for Socialism: Soviet Criticisms of*

China (Princeton, NJ: Princeton University Press, 1985), and his *The Chinese Debate About Soviet Socialism, 1978–1985* (Princeton, NJ: Princeton University Press, 1987).

25. See the very favorable description of the "Stalin Five Year Plan" of 1946–1950 in *Shehui zhuyi bisai zai Sulian* [Socialist competition in the Soviet Union] (Beiping: Zhongwai chubanshe, 1949), pp. 97–112. Also see Leonard Schapiro, *The Communist Party of the Soviet Union* (New York: Vintage Books, 1971), p. 510.

26. See, for instance, New China News Agency, Daily News Report, November 8, 1950, pp. 60–62.

27. *Suliande gongren* [Soviet workers] (Shanghai: Laodong chubanshe, 1951), p. 20.

28. *Gongren wenhua keben* [Culture textbook for workers] (Shanghai: Lianhe chubanshe, 1950), vol. 2, p. 24.

29. Qian Gufeng, *Sidalin pailaide ren* [The men whom Stalin sent] (Shanghai: Laodong chubanshe, 1953), p. 2.

30. *Suliande gongren*, p. 20.

31. Zhu Cishou, *Gongchan laodong jingji* [The economics of factory labor] (Shanghai: Lixin huiji tushu yongpinshe chuban, 1951), p. 23.

32. The CCP's handbooks for its members emphasized the importance of relying on the Communist Party for most matters. See *Gongchandang yuande keben* [Communist party member textbook] (Dongan: Dongbeiju xuanchuanbu, 1947), p. 1.

33. Zhou Ming, "Notes from a Visit to a Moscow Knitting Factory," *Gongren ribao*, December 2, 1949, p. 5.

34. New China News Agency, Daily News Release, June 1, 1950, p. 5.

35. Zhao Dexin, ed., *Gongren jieji he gongchandang* [The working class and the Communist party] (Beijing: Gongren chubanshe, 1952), pp. 26–44.

36. *Zhongguo gongye* [Chinese industry] 2, no. 5 (1950).

37. Zhou Ming, "Notes," p. 5.

38. Khrushchev's feelings about Mao are probably fairly representative of the Soviet leadership. In his memoirs, he says, among other things, that "Mao Tse-tung has played politics with Asiatic cunning, following his own rules of cajolery, treachery, savage vengeance, and deceit." In *Khrushchev Remembers* (Boston: Little, Brown, 1970), p. 461.

39. Many Soviet specialist have casually mentioned this, but it is explicitly stated in Volkogonov's recent biography of Stalin. See his *Stalin: Triumph and Tragedy*, p. 540.

40. Many believe that Stalin was pursuing a "weak neighbor policy" in China, since a powerless China would be more likely to accept Soviet influence. See Steven I. Levine, *Anvil of Victory: The Communist Revolution in Manchuria, 1945–1948* (New York: Columbia University Press, 1987), pp. 26–33.

41. See the interview with L. Delyusin in *USSR–China in the Changing World* (Moscow: Novosti Press Agency Publishing House, 1989), p. 53.

42. Author's interview with one of Mao Zedong's Russian interpreters who accompanied him to Moscow, Beijing, 1988.

43. According to a newly published Bo Yibo memoir, Mao felt humiliated that Stalin would not see him immediately. Bo writes that at the end of December 1949, Mao became very angry and threw a fit. See Bo Yibo,

Ruogan zhongde juece yu shijian de huigu [A review of some very important policies and events], vol. 1: 1949–1956 (Beijing: Zhonggong zhongyang dangxiao chubanshe, 1991), p. 41.

44. N. Fedorenko, "The Stalin–Mao Summit in Moscow," *Far Eastern Affairs* 2 (1989):134–148; Shi Zhe, "I Accompanied Chairman Mao." *Far Eastern Affairs* 2 (1989):125–133.

45. The first reported meeting between the two governments took place on January 2, 1950, when Mao met with Molotov and Mikoyan. In Mao's telegram to the CCP Central Committee about Sino-Soviet negotiations on that day, he noted that Stalin had agreed that Zhou Enlai should come to Moscow for the negotiations, but there is no explicit mention of a meeting between Mao and Stalin personally. See Mao's telegram dated January 2–3, 1950, in *Jianguo yilai Mao Zedong wengao* [Mao Zedong communications from the founding of the PRC], vol. 1: September 1949–December 1950 (Beijing: Zhongyang wenxian chushe, 1990), pp. 211–13.

46. Wladimir S. Merzalov, ed., *Biographic Dictionary of the USSR* (Munich: Institute for the Study of the USSR, 1958; English ed., New York: Scarecrow Press, 1958).

47. For a summary of such work, see "Report by Kao Kang at the First Conference of Representatives of the Chinese Communist Party in the Northeast," *Current Background,* August 23, 1950 (Hong Kong: American Consulate General, 1950).

48. See various issues of *People's China* (Beijing: Foreign Language Press) for the years 1950 to 1952, for an idea of the type of Soviet delegation sent.

49. This is my translation of a list found in the 1955 *Zhongguo zong shumu* [Chinese general title catalogue], pp. 1164–69.

50. A more complete list of the Soviet books can be found in note 14 in this chapter.

51. W. J. F. Jenner persuasively argues that China's tyrannical past influences all of its policies and actions and that Marxism-Leninism just extended and modified the traditional attitudes toward the past instead of replacing them. See his *The Tyranny of History: The Roots of China's Crisis* (London: Allen Lane, 1992).

Chapter 2

1. This is a neglected period of Soviet history that is often sandwiched between accounts of the war and the rise of Khrushchev. There are few book-length treatments of the period, but fortunately there are at least chapters devoted to Soviet society in the postwar period. See Jerry Hough and Merle Fainsod, *How the Soviet Union Is Governed* (Cambridge, MA: Harvard University Press, 1979); Robert H. McNeal, *Stalin: Man and Ruler* (London: Macmillan, 1988); Roy A. Medvedev, *Let History Judge,* trans. Colleen Taylor (New York: Vintage Books, 1971); Leonard Schapiro, *The Communist Party of the Soviet Union* (New York: Vintage Books, 1971).

2. According to official Soviet calculations, 1,710 towns and other workers' settlements, more than 70,000 villages, and more than 6 million buildings were burned or destroyed; 32,000 industrial enterprises, 65,000 kilometers of railroad line, and thousands of collective and state farms were

damaged. See L. S. Rogachevskaya, *Sotsialisticheskoe sorevnovanie v SSSR; istoricheskie ocherki* [Socialist competition in the USSR; historical studies] (Moscow: Nauka, 1977), p. 213. See *Pravda*, September 13, 1945, for losses in Soviet industry.

3. Eugene Zaleski, *Stalinist Planning for Economic Growth, 1933–1952* (Chapel Hill: University of North Carolina Press, 1980), p. 346.

4. The regions under German occupation suffered the highest losses. In Ukraine the figures were 65.3 percent and 48 percent, and in Belorussia, 53.7 percent and 38.6 percent, respectively, of the prewar level. *Vostanovlenie narodnogo khozyaistva SSSR. Sozdanie ekonomiki razvitogo sotsializma. 1946–nachalo 1960-kh godov* [Restoration of the national economy of the USSR. The creation of an economy of developed socialism. 1946–the beginning of the 1960s], vol. 6 (Moscow: Nauka, 1980), p. 32.

5. The more familiar CPSU is used as an abbreviation for the Communist Party of the Soviet Union throughout this book, although technically in the 1940s the Communist Party was known as the VKP (b), or the All-Union Communist Party (bolsheviks).

6. The work on the Fourth Five-Year Plan actually began long before the war had ended. Already in August 1945, the Politburo had ordered the State Planning Agency, Gosplan USSR, to begin working on a technical plan of reconstruction for the economy for all republics, regions and counties. See *Pravda*, August 19, 1945.

7. N. S. Maslova, *Proizvoditel'nost' truda v promyshlennosti SSSR* [Labor productivity in industry in the USSR] (Moscow: Gosudarstvennoe izdatel'stvo politicheskoi literatury, 1949), pp. 63–64.

8. See Cynthia S. Kaplan's excellent review, "The Impact of World War II on the Party," *in The Impact of World War II on the Soviet Union*, ed. Susan J. Linz (Totowa, NJ: Rowman & Allanheld, 1985), pp. 157–88.

9. For descriptions of earlier systems of management in Soviet industry, see Joseph S. Berliner, *Factory and Manager in the USSR* (Cambridge, MA: Harvard University Press, 1957); David Granick, *Managerial Comparisons of Four Developed Countries: France, Britain, United States and Russia* (Cambridge, MA: MIT Press, 1972) and David Granick, *The Red Executive* (Garden City, NY: Doubleday, 1961); Leopold Haimson, "Decision-making and Communications in Soviet Industry." *Studies in Soviet Communication*, vol. 2. (Cambridge, MA: MIT Center for International Studies, 1952).

10. M. I. Khlusov, *Promyshlennost' i rabochii klass SSSR, 1946–1950; dokumenty i materialy* [Industry and the working class in the USSR, 1946–1950; documents and materials] (Moscow: Nauka, 1989), p. 177.

11. M. I. Khlusov, *Razvitie sovetskoi industrii 1946–1958* [The development of Soviet industry, 1946–1958] (Moscow: Nauka, 1977), p. 90.

12. Ibid., pp. 90–92.

13. This type of recruitment had been extensively used during the 1930s and refers to the organized effort to recruit laborers from the collective farms to work under contract in industry.

14. Sheila Fitzpatrick, "Postwar Soviet Society: The 'Return to Normalcy', 1945–1953," in *The Impact of World War II on the Soviet Union*, ed. Susan J. Linz (Totowa, NJ: Rowman & Allanheld, 1985), pp. 129–56.

15. For instance, Naum Jasny estimates that the more than 2 million German war prisoners represented about 10 percent of the total hired labor in material production in the immediate postwar period. See Naum Jasny, *Soviet Industrialization 1928–1952* (Chicago: University of Chicago Press, 1961), pp. 246–47.

16. See S. G. Wheatcroft, "On Assessing the Size of Forced Concentration Camp Labour in the Soviet Union 1929–1956," *Soviet Studies* 33 (April 1981): 267–68, cited by Fitzpatrick, "Postwar Soviet Society," p. 142.

17. Fitzpatrick, "Postwar Soviet Society," p. 143.

18. Khlusov, *Promyshlennost'*, pp. 188–89.

19. Ibid., pp. 193–95.

20. Maslova (*Proizvoditel'nost'*, p. 174) discusses the decree entitled "On the responsibility of workers and employees of enterprises of military production for unauthorized leave from the job."

21. R. Fakiolis, "Problems of Labour Mobility in the USSR," *Soviet Studies* 14 (July 1962):17, quoted in Fitzpatrick, *Postwar Soviet Society*, p. 141.

22. See Jerzy Gliksman, *Postwar Trends in Soviet Labor Policy*, RAND Research Memorandum no. P-754 (Santa Monica, CA: RAND Corporation, 1955), for a review of both the legislation and its enforcement.

23. It is probable that at least some of the migrating workers show up in the statistics as recruits in other programs. Unfortunately, there are no data either to support or to refute this.

24. The USSR Ministry of Education also trained many youths who had been orphaned during the war and were living in orphanages at the end of the war. Khlusov claims (Khlusov, *Razvitie*, pp. 95–96) that in 1949, 28,100 young men and women received a technical education and entered the industrial workforce.

25. Khlusov (*Razvitie*, p. 98) presents an annual breakdown, based on archival research, of workers trained in these industries.

26. See, for instance, *People's Daily*, October 26, 1950, on the economic achievements of the USSR during the Fourth Five-Year Plan, trans. New China News Agency, *Daily News Release*, October 27, 1950, p. 207. In the early 1950s such articles were also frequently printed in the front section of *Zhongguo gongye* [Chinese industry] (Shanghai: Zhongguo gongye yuekanshe, 1950).

27. This was the "Summary Report on Implementing the Fourth Five-Year Plan of 1946–1950." See Chapter 1 of this book for a complete list of works that the Soviets translated into Chinese.

28. This section on fulfillment of the Five-Year Plan relies on Zaleski, *Stalinist Planning*, pp. 345–402.

29. Warren Nutter calculated that the production of all Soviet industry increased 21.7 percent in 1947 over 1946. See Warren G. Nutter, *Growth of Industrial Production in the Soviet Union* (Princeton, NJ: Princeton University Press, 1962). Cited in Zaleski, *Stalinist Planning*, p. 367.

30. During the summer of 1947, Gosplan USSR proposed that a new fifteen-year plan be drawn up. Meetings and conferences were held, and documents were drafted, but this effort, too, was ultimately abandoned (see Zaleski, *Stalinist Planning*, p. 386, for details).

31. *Kommunisticheskaya partiya sovetskogo soyuza v rezolyutsiyakh i reshen-*

iyakh s"ezdov, konferentsiy i plenumov TsK [The Communist Party of the Soviet Union in resolutions and decisions of congresses, conferences and plenums of the Central Committee], vol. 8: 1946–1955 (Moscow: Izdatel'stvo politicheskoy literatury, 1985), pp. 17–20.

32. Ibid., p. 17.

33. It ordered socialist competitions to be organized among workers and among enterprises, collective farms, villages, cities, regions, counties, and republics (*Kommunisticheskaya partiya*, p. 18).

34. Ibid., p. 19.

35. Ibid., p. 20.

36. These would be courses in labor motivation, named for the famous Soviet labor hero of the 1930s, Alexei Stakhanov.

37. Khlusov, *Promyshlennost'*, pp. 28–31.

38. N. Chernyak, *Partiinaya organizatsiya i sotsialisticheskoe sorevnovanie* [The party organization and socialist competition] (Moscow: Moskovskii rabochii, 1948).

39. Ibid., pp. 26–35.

40. Berliner, *Factory and Manager*, pp. 264–71.

41. In earlier periods, Soviet officials often complained that the extent and achievements of socialist competition were exaggerated. See Lewis H. Siegelbaum, *Stakhanovism and the Politics of Productivity in the USSR, 1935–1941* (Cambridge: Cambridge University Press, 1988) for a complete account of socialist competition in the prewar period. The charges of inflating the numbers in competitions are discussed on pp. 48–49.

42. *Istoriya sotsialisticheskogo sorevnovaniya v SSSR* [The history of socialist competition in the USSR] (Moscow: Profizdat, 1980), p. 151.

43. Kaplan, "The Impact," p. 161.

44. N. B. Lebedeva, *Partiinoe rukovodstvo sotsialisticheskim sorevnovaniem; istoriya i sovremennost'* [Party leadership of socialist competition; history and contemporaneity] (Leningrad: Lenizdat, 1979), p. 157.

45. Kaplan, "The Impact," p. 160.

46. Fang Shu, *Campaign of Party-Expansion of the Chinese Communist Party in 1952* (Hong Kong: Union Research Institute, 1954).

47. Ibid.

48. Chernyak, *Partiinaya*, p. 10.

49. Ibid., p. 6.

50. Ibid., p. 7.

51. Ibid., p. 9.

52. See the chapters on Stakhanovitism and the use of "Kovalyev's methods" in industry in Zhu Cishou, ed., *Gongchang laodong jingji* [The economics of factory labor] (Shanghai: Liyanhui jituanshu yongpinshe, 1951), pp. 195–205.

53. This was the first time that so-called social issues (education, systematic technical training, etc.) were included as goals for competition. Traditionally the workers had competed only on the basis of production targets. See Rogachevskaya, *Sotsialisticheskoe*, p. 222.

54. *Pravda*, May 15, 1946.

55. *Leningradskaya pravda*, February 8, 1947.

56. Rogachevskaya, *Sotsialisticheskoe*, p. 225.

57. See *Foreign Broadcast Information Service, February* 26, 1947; March 14, 1947.

58. Ibid., February 26, 1947.

59. Chernyak, *Partiinaya*, pp. 15–16.

60. The drive to rationalize, known as *helihua* in Chinese, began to sweep China's industries as early as 1950.

61. Rogachevskaya, *Sotsialisticheskoe*, pp. 227–28.

62. Ibid., pp. 230–31.

63. *Istoriya sotsialisticheskogo sorevnovaniya*, p. 145.

64. Khlusov, *Razvitie*, p. 199.

65. Chernyak, *Partiinaya*, pp. 16–17.

66. That is roughly 3 million industrial workers out of a population of approximately 536.4 million. See John S. Aird, "Recent Demographic Data from China: Problems and Prospects," in Joint Economic Committee, *China Under the Four Modernizations*, pt. 1 (Washington, DC: U.S. Government Printing Office, 1982), p. 178; *Ten Great Years: Statistics of the Economic and Cultural Achievements of the People's Republic of China* (Peking: Foreign Languages Press), p. 183.

Chapter 3

1. See Suzanne Pepper, "The KMT–CCP Conflict 1945–1949," in *Republican China 1912–1949, Part II*, ed. John K. Fairbank and Albert Feuerwerker, vol. 13 of *The Cambridge History of China* (Cambridge: Cambridge University Press, 1986), pp. 723–82.

2. These include William Brugger, *Democracy and Organisation in the Chinese Industrial Enterprise (1948–1953)* (Cambridge: Cambridge University Press, 1976); Jean Chesneaux, *The Chinese Labor Movement, 1919–1927*, trans. H. M. Wright (Stanford, CA: Stanford University Press, 1968); Charles Hoffman, *The Chinese Worker* (Albany: State University of New York Press, 1974); Shao-er Ong, *Labor Problems in Communist China (to February 1953)*. Studies in Chinese Communism Series III, no. 5 (Lackland Air Force Base, TX: U.S. Air Force Personnel and Training Research Center, 1955); Andrew G. Walder, *Communist Neo-Traditionalism; Work and Authority in Chinese Industry* (Berkeley and Los Angeles: University of California Press, 1986). Recent Western labor scholarship has tended to be regional: See Gail Hershatter, *The Workers of Tianjin, 1900–1949* (Stanford, CA: Stanford University Press, 1986); Emily Honig, *Sisters and Strangers; Women in the Shanghai Cotton Mills, 1919–1949* (Stanford, CA: Stanford University Press, 1986); Kenneth G. Lieberthal, *Revolution and Tradition in Tientsin, 1949–1952* (Stanford, CA: Stanford University Press, 1980); Ezra Vogel, *Canton Under Communism* (New York: Harper & Row, 1969).

3. See Lucian Bianco, *Origins of the Chinese Revolution, 1915–1949*, trans. Muriel Bell (Stanford, CA: Stanford University Press, 1971), p. 84.

4. See T. N. Akatova, *Rabochee dvizheniye v gomin'danovskom Kitae 1927–1937 gg.* [The workers' movement in Guomindang China, 1927–1937] (Moscow: Nauka, 1983); L. P. Delyusin, *Rabochee dvizheniye v Kitae, nankinskii*

gomin'dan i rabochii vopros (1927–1931) [The workers' movement in China; the Nanjing Guomindang and the labor question (1927–1931)] (Moscow: Nauka, 1982); V. G. Gel'bras, ed., *Rabochii klass Kitaya (1949–1974 gg.)* [The working class of China, 1949–1974] (Moscow: Nauka, 1978); A. I. Kartunova, *Politika kompartii Kitaya v rabochem voprose nakanune revolyutsii 1925–1927* [The policies of the Communist party of China in the worker's question on the eve of the revolution, 1925–1927] (Moscow: Nauka, 1983); V. I. Khor'kov, *Nankinskii gomin'dan i rabochii vopros, 1927–1932* [The Nanjing Guomindang and the worker question, 1927–1932] (Moscow: Nauka, 1977); A. Lozovskii, *Rabochii Kitai v 1927 godu; sbornik statei* [China's worker in 1927; handbook of articles]. (Moscow: Profintern, 1928).

5. Brugger, *Democracy and Organisation,* p. 37.

6. V. G. Gel'bras, *Sotsial'no-politicheskaya struktura KNR 50–60e gody* [Social and political structure of the PRC in the 1950s and 1960s] (Moscow: Nauka, 1980), p. 25.

7. Brugger maintains in *Democracy and Organisation* (p. 3) that the Chinese working class never reached a "bourgeois" stage in terms of collective consciousness and instead would have to be labeled vaguely "middle class" in 1949.

8. This was the situation even into the 1950s. In 1953, for instance, 70 percent (105,000 out of 150,000) of the enterprises had fewer than 10 workers; 30 percent had 10 or more; and only 1.3 percent had more than 100 workers. See Gel'bras, *Sotsial'no-politicheskaya,* p. 41.

9. This was a particularly troublesome point from the perspective of Marxist–Leninist theory, as Gel'bras points out in *Sotsial'no-politicheskaya,* p. 41.

10. Ibid., p. 40.

11. Ibid., p. 42.

12. Z. A. Muromtseva, *Problemy industrializatsii Kitaiskoi narodnoi respubliki* [Problems of industrialization in the Chinese People's Republic] (Moscow: Nauka, 1971), p. 111.

13. The gang bosses also often supervised the laborers (during work and leisure time) after hiring them, paid their wages, and provided housing and food. Brugger provides an excellent summary of their duties and responsibilities in his discussion in *Democracy and Organisation,* pp. 42–47. Also, for an illuminating account of the work of the gang boss system, see Stephen Andors, ed., *Workers and Workplaces in Revolutionary China,* The China Book Project, Translation and Commentary (White Plains, NY: M. E. Sharpe, 1977).

14. Hershatter, *The Workers,* p. 144.

15. D. K. Lieu, *China's Economic Stabilization and Reconstruction* (New Brunswick, NJ: Rutgers University Press, 1948), p. 55.

16. All the Soviet sources in this section are listed as Chinese translations in chap. 4 of the *Zhongguo zong shumu* [Chinese general title catalogue] (Beijing: Xinhua shudian biandian, 1955), pp. 123–27, in the section entitled "Industrial Management."

17. This discussion covers only the management of state enterprises and firms (i.e., not cooperatives) in all sectors of industry.

18. A. F. Rumyantsev, *Organizatsiya upravleniya promyshlennost'yu SSSR* [The organization of industrial management in the USSR] (Moscow: Vyshaya partiinaya shkola pri TsK KPSS, 1953), pp. 9–10.

19. A. Arakelian, *Industrial Management in the USSR*, trans. Ellsworth L. Raymond (Washington, DC: Public Affairs Press, 1950), p. 90.

20. The idea that "the personal interests of members of society can be satisfied by universal expansion to socialist production" (Arakelian, *Industrial Management*, p. 87) was a concept also stressed by the Chinese communists in their early work. See Willy Kraus, *Economic Development and Social Change in the People's Republic of China*, trans. E. M. Holz (New York: Springer-Verlag, 1982), pp. 8–9.

21. The "right of control" (*pravo kontrolya*) is sometimes translated as the "right of verification." See Jerry Hough, *The Soviet Prefects* (Cambridge, MA: Harvard University Press, 1969), pp. 87–100, for an excellent discussion of the "right of control."

22. See Arakelian, *Industrial Management*, p. 92.

23. The Soviet authors stressed the differences between capitalist and socialist practices. Under capitalism, the manager (as a proxy for the owner), worked only for his own profit. Under socialism, the goals of the manager coincided with the goals of all of the workers: to develop socialism, to strengthen the country's defense, and to improve the cultural and material conditions of all workers. In this way, the manager simultaneously satisfied his own needs and those of the state (Arakelian, *Industrial Management*, p. 87). The socialist manager was a servant of the people (not of the capitalist owner) and hence represented the interests of all Soviet citizens. See Sh. L. Rozenfel'd, *Organizatsiya upravleniya promyshlennost'yu SSSR* [The organization of industrial management in the USSR] (Moscow: Gosplanizdat, 1950), p. 25.

24. Rozenfel'd, *Organizatsiya*, p. 29.

25. The Soviet handbooks noted that the Party's involvement not only strengthened the system of one-man management but also increased the Party's authority at the enterprise. See D. Goginava, *Partiinii kontrol' na predpriyatii* [Party control in the enterprise] (Moscow: Gospolitizdat, 1949), p. 3.

26. Rozenfel'd, *Organizatsiya*, pp. 32–33.

27. Arakelian, *Industrial Management*, p. 166.

28. Rozenfel'd, *Organizatsiya*, pp. 34–36; Rumyantsev, *Organizatsiya*, pp. 16–18.

29. Arakelian, *Industrial Management*, p. 94.

30. The manager's official role concerning the labor force was largely pro forma. For a description of the manager's other functions in a Soviet enterprise, see Joseph S. Berliner, *Factory and Manager in the USSR* (Cambridge, MA: Harvard University Press, 1957); David Granick, *Management of the Industrial Firm in the USSR: A Study in Soviet Economic Planning* (New York: Columbia University Press, 1954); and David Granick, *The Red Executive: A Study of the Organization Man in Russian Industry* (Garden City, NY: Doubleday, 1961).

31. Every enterprise, organization, and factory with at least three Party members could form a primary Party organization. If the primary Party organization consisted of more than fifteen members, they could elect a bureau, and in the larger institutions, they elected one or more Party secretaries. According to the Party's rules, only those institutions with a hundred or more members could have a paid, full-time party secretary. The primary Party organizations were located at the place of work; however, it is important to remember that they were subordinate to the city or district Party com-

mittees, not to the director or the enterprise. See Jerry F. Hough and Merle Fainsod, *How the Soviet Union Is Governed* (Cambridge, MA: Harvard University Press, 1979), pp. 354–61; and Leonard Schapiro, *The Communist Party of the Soviet Union*, 2nd ed. (New York: Vintage Books, 1971), pp. 448–49.

32. Rumyantsev, *Organizatsiya*, p. 42.

33. During this period, the labor union claimed that nearly 99 percent of all Soviet workers belonged to the union (Goginava, *Partiinii kontrol'*, p. 68).

34. Ibid., p. 67.

35. The authors of the management handbooks state that the Party organization did not completely control the production process; it only guaranteed for the manager that the entire collective fulfilled the plan. The Party was not to replace the director, because this would violate one-man management (Rumyantsev, *Organizatsiya*, p. 43). However, the Party was supposed to be the one body that always approached problems from the general "Party and state viewpoint" (Arakelian, *Industrial Management*, p. 157).

36. Arakelian, *Industrial Management*, p. 156.

37. Storming (*shturmirovanie*) was an irregular work regime that many enterprises adopted. During the first two to three weeks of the month, little or no work was done in the enterprise, which therefore made it necessary to "storm" in order to complete a month's work in the last eight to ten days.

38. Goginava, *Partiinii kontrol'*, pp. 11–15.

39. Ibid., p. 32.

40. Arakelian, *Industrial Management*, p. 158.

41. Goginava, *Partiinii kontrol'*, p. 66.

42. Agitators (*agitatory*) were regular workers and foremen who propagandized among the workers for the Communist Party in the factory.

43. V. N. Shchepanskii, *Massogo-politicheskaya rabota na zavode* [Mass-political work at the factory] (Moscow: Gospolitizdat, 1949), pp. 34–41.

44. Ibid., p. 27.

45. Goginava, *Partiinii kontrol'*, pp. 53–55.

46. Shchepanskii, *Massogo-politicheskaya rabota*, pp. 34–40.

47. Rumyantsev, *Organizatsiya*, p. 45.

48. O. Kremnyeva, *Opyt politicheskoi agitatsii na predpriyatii* [The experience of political agitation in the enterprise] (Moscow: Gospolitizdat, 1948), p. 5.

49. Ibid., pp. 6–13.

50. According to the handbooks, the latter was the most popular topic at meetings because everybody wanted to be a model worker (Kremnyeva, *Opyt*, pp. 16–20).

51. In such cases, the planning department would rework the norms to show individual goals, and a book was brought out in which each foreman could record his workers' plan fulfillment by month, year, and five-year plan.

52. Kremnyeva, *Opyt*, pp. 21–22.

53. Goginava, *Partiinii kontrol'*, p. 29.

54. Kremnyeva, *Opyt*, pp. 23–25.

55. Goginava, *Partiinii kontrol'*, p. 29.

56. Kremnyeva, *Opyt*, p. 27.

57. Ibid., pp. 30–33.

58. For the significance of the written word as propaganda, see V. Murachev and M. Koshonina, *Naglyadnaya agitatsiya na predpriyatii* [Visual agitation at the enterprise] (Moscow: Gospolitizdat, 1953).

59. Goginava, *Partiinii kontrol'*, p. 31; Shchepanskii, *Massogo-politicheskaya rabota*, pp. 22–25.

60. Shchepanskii, *Massogo-politicheskaya rabota*, p. 23.

61. Goginava, *Partiinii kontrol'*, p. 31.

62. Bolshevik qualities were exactingness, high principles, and an intolerance of shortcomings, conceit, and self-satisfaction (ibid., p. 59).

63. Ibid., p. 32.

64. Shchepanskii, *Massogo-politicheskaya rabota*, p. 22.

65. Kremnyeva, *Opyt*, pp. 36–40.

66. Ibid., pp. 49–55.

67. A. Zhuravlev, *Agitator—organizator sotsialisticheskogo sorevnovaniya* [The agitator is the organizor of socialist competition] (Moscow: Gospolitizdat, 1948), p. 3.

68. For an excellent discussion of the origins of "socialist competitions" and "shock brigades" in the Soviet Union, see Hiroaki Kuromiya, *Stalin's Industrial Revolution: Politics and Workers, 1928–1932* (Cambridge: Cambridge University Press, 1988), pp. 115–19.

69. Zhuravlyev, *Agitator*, p. 5.

70. Ibid., p. 6.

71. Ibid., p. 11.

72. A very good overview of the phenomenon of "Stakhanovism" can be found in Lewis H. Siegelbaum, *Stakhanovism and the Politics of Productivity in the USSR, 1935–1941* (Cambridge: Cambridge University Press, 1988).

73. Shchepanskii, *Massogo-politicheskaya rabota*, p. 45.

74. This was not new, either. Stakhanov himself wrote a biography in 1937, entitled *Rasskaz o moyei zhizni* [The story of my life], which was distributed widely at the time.

75. The director was supposed to attend so that he could say which proposals could or could not be carried out. (If he rejected a proposal, he had to justify his actions). If the director could not attend the production conference, according to an authoritative labor union manual, he was required to acquaint himself with the production conference's proposals the next day and submit a written note to the effect that he would ensure their fulfillment. See P. Mogilenko and V. Zasetskii, *Organizatsiya raboty proizvodstvennykh soveshchanii* [Organizational work of the production conference] (Moscow: Profizdat, 1950), p. 14.

76. Ibid., p. 13.

77. Criticism and self-criticism were the labor union's tools at the conferences. The workers, the foremen, and even the manager had to stand up and criticize their own work performance and the organization of the plant's work in general, if necessary. This was thought to help inspire workers to be more vigilant and productive and to make management more responsible.

78. I. I. Voronkov, ed., *Ekonomika i organizatsiya proizvodstva* [Economics and organization of production] (Moscow and Sverdlovsk: Gosudarstvennoe nauchno-tekhnicheskoe izdatel'stvo machinostroitel'noi literatury, 1954), pp. 63–64.

79. A 1921 law provided for coverage in the cases of temporary or permanent disability. See Arakelian, *Industrial Management*, pp. 166–67.)

80. Ibid., p. 162.

Chapter 4

1. For a discussion of the Communist takeover of Beijing, see A. Doak Barnett, *China on the Eve of Communist Takeover* (1963; Boulder, CO: Westview Press, 1985), pp. 315–57; for the takeover of Tianjin, see Kenneth G. Liberthal, *Revolution and Tradition in Tientsin, 1949–1952* (Stanford, CA: Stanford University Press, 1980), pp. 28–52; for the takeover of Guangdong province, see Ezra Vogel, *Canton Under Communism* (1969; New York: Harper & Row, 1971), pp. 41–90. For a description of the takeover of industry, see William Brugger, *Democracy and Organisation in the Chinese Enterprise (1948–1953)* (Cambridge: Cambridge University Press, 1976).

2. Some Soviets have claimed credit for the "Manchurian success" in industrial management. One early source, for instance, strongly makes the case that the Chinese in Manchuria learned "the rudiments of economic management" from the jointly administered Changchun Railroad. See G. V. Astafyev, *China's Economic Problems* (Bombay: People's Publishing House, 1950), pp. 34–35. In reality, the number of Soviets involved was miniscule when compared with the size and population of Manchuria.

3. It turned out that the democracy movement, which was brought "from above" to the masses, was not easily implemented. Chen Yongwen, the author of an authoritative industrial management text, explained that after liberation in the northeast, in some factories the relationship among the Party, the administration, and the trade union was "not harmonious." In such cases, he said, it was necessary to "launch a democracy campaign" (*fadong minzhu yundong*), during which time the administrative management cadres were to, on the basis of criticism and self-criticism, create a factory management committee. See Chen Yongwen, *Gongchang guanli minzhuhua wenti jianghua* [Discussion of problems of factory management democratization] (Beijing: Gongren chubanshe yinxing, 1950), p. 5.

4. See Bai Yuan and Bai Shi, trans. and eds., "Problems of the Mass–Party Relationship in the Enterprise," *Xuexi sulian qiye gongzuo jingyan* [We study the Soviet experience in enterprise work] (Beijing: Dazhong shudian chuban, 1950); Central Heavy Industrial Ministry's Personnel Office, Labor and Wages Department, ed. and trans., *Gangtie gongye de laodong zuzhi* [Labor organizations in the iron and steel industry] (Beijing: Kexue jishu chubanshe, 1952); Wu Qingyou, *Suliande gongye guanli* [Soviet industrial management] (Shanghai: Zhonghua shuju yinxing, 1950); as well as hundreds of articles in journals such as *Zhongguo gongye* [Chinese industry] and newspapers like *Laodong bao* [Workers' daily].

5. See Hu Lintai, ed., *Suixin gongchang guanli fa* [The newest factory management methods] (Tianjin: Yizhi shudian, 1951); Hu Shiru and Liu Wenju, eds., *Gongye qiye shengchang zuzhi yu guanli* [Organization and management of industrial enterprises and factories] (Shanghai: Liyanhui tushe yongpinshe chuban, 1953); Shi Liang, ed., *Gongchang guanli gailun* [An introduction to factory management] (Shanghai: Liyanhui tushe yongpinshe

chuban, 1952); *Women zenyang guanli qiye* [How we manage an enterprise] (Beijing: Gongren chubanshe, 1951); Zhu Cishou, ed., *Gongchang laodong jingji* [The economics of factory labor] (Shanghai: Liyanhui jituanshu yongpinshe, 1951).

6. This section relies on the one management handbook that presents the entire Chinese "management mechanism" ideas in the most systematic fashion: Shiru and Liu Wenju, eds., *Gongye qiye*, pp. 153–91.

7. Ibid., pp. 153–55.

8. Ibid., pp. 185–89.

9. The Chinese text quotes Stalin as saying that merely picking the right cadres for the right jobs is not enough. Their work must be supervised every day, and there must be systematic checks to ensure that all resolutions are implemented.

10. Hu Shiru and Liu Wenju, eds., *Gongye qiye*, pp. 165–68.

11. Ibid., pp. 163–65.

12. The Soviet literature on socialist competition is enormous. For Soviet documents about the postwar Stakhanovite movement, see M. I. Khlusov, ed., *Promyshlennost' i rabochii klass SSSR 1946–1950* [Industry and the working class in the USSR, 1946–1950] (Moscow: Nauka, 1989). For an extensive Soviet bibliography on the phenomenon of Stakhanovism, see V. A. Sakharov, *Zarozhdenie i razvitie stakhanovskogo dvizheniya* [The origin and development of the Stakhanovite movement] (Moscow: Izdatel'stvo Moskovsogo universiteta, 1985).

13. The Chinese stressed, just as the Soviets did, that in a capitalist system, new management techniques were always secret but that in a socialist system, the work of each worker and of each enterprise was not private, but an affair of society and even of the nation.

14. In the Communist experience, the Stakhanovite competition had a special role in production. Therefore, one of the functions of the enterprise management mechanism was to organize collective Stakhanovite work at the factory. For Western descriptions of the history of Stakhanovism, see Hiroaki Kuromiya, *Stalin's Industrial Revolution; Politics and Workers, 1928–1932* (Cambridge: Cambridge University Press, 1988); and Lewis H. Siegelbaum, *Stakhanovism and the Politics of Productivity in the USSR, 1935–1941* (Cambridge: Cambridge University Press, 1988).

15. Hu Shiru and Liu Wenju, eds., *Gongye qiye*, pp. 157–63.

16. Ibid., pp. 182–85.

17. Ibid., pp. 168–77.

18. Ibid., pp. 189–91.

19. Ibid., pp. 177–81.

20. Ibid., pp. 155–57.

21. See press reports as translated in *Current Background*, August 23, 1950, p. 14.

22. See Chen Yongwen, *Gongchang guanli*, p. 2.

23. See, for instance, Ai Mu et al., *Zenyang lingdao gongchang* [How to manage a factory] (Dalian: Dalian dazhong shudian yinxing, 1947); Deng Fadeng, *Lun gongying gongchang* [On the state-owned factory] (Dongbei: Dongbei shudian, 1946); Guan Shuixin, "Three Years of the Economic Construction in the Northeast," *Zhongguo gongye* [Chinese industry], vol. 1, no. 1

(March) (Shanghai: Zhongguo gongye yuekan she, 1950), pp. 18–22; Tao Fen, *Shiye guanli yu zhiye xiuyang* [Enterprise management and occupational training] (Beijing: Shenghuo, dushu, xinzhi sanlian shudian, 1950). See also frequent articles in workers' newspapers such as "Factory Management Must Democratize Before Furthering the Benefits to Labor and Capital," *Laodong bao* [Workers' daily], July 9, 1949, p. 3.

24. See press reports as translated in *Current Background*, August 23, 1950, and others. The northeast experience was widely disseminated in China in the late 1940s and early 1950s in newspapers and early management handbooks.

25. See *Women zenyang*, 1951.

26. Chen Yongwen, *Gongchang guanli*, pp. 27–33.

27. *Women zenyang*, p. 5.

28. Ibid., pp. 8–9.

29. In the newly liberated areas, the FMC standing committee instituted "military control" (*junshi quanzhi*). In these cases, the military representative who was posted to the factory was included as a member of both the FMC and its standing committee. See Hu Shiru and Liu Wenju, eds., *Gongye qiye*, p. 23.

30. Ibid., p. 23.

31. This was known as "relying on the masses," as Beijing Motor Repair Plant director Song Beichong explained. At his factory, the FMC worked on resolving wage disputes. See *Women zenyang*, pp. 19–21.

32. Ibid., pp. 13–14.

33. Although the FEWC was administered by the labor union, it had no power to elect labor union representatives or to change the labor union rules. This could be done only by decision of the entire body of the labor union. See *Gongyun wenti yibaige* [One hundred questions on the workers' movement] pt. 1 (Beijing: Gongren chubanshe yinxing, 1950), p. 46.

34. See *Gongyun wenti*, p. 45.

35. *Women zenyang*, p. 5.

36. Ibid., p. 1.

37. Ibid., pp. 5–6.

38. Ibid., p. 6.

39. Ibid., p. 7.

40. Ibid., p. 23.

41. Ibid., pp. 17–18.

42. See *Current Background*, August 23, 1950, p. 15.

43. Chen Yongwen, *Gongchang guanli*, pp. 11–12.

44. The early Chinese handbooks answered no. Under the system of one-man management, the manager was responsible for good management and for increasing production; if production were poor, then the state would hold him responsible. The FMC was the vehicle through which the director could rely on all workers and employees as "masters" to work hard voluntarily and increase production. In this way both the workers and the manager were responsible for the production results. See Chen Yongwen, *Gongchang guanli*, p. 14.

45. Many Chinese scholars told me this in interviews conducted in Beijing in 1988, and even Soviet scholars now admit it. See the interviews

with Soviet scholars A. V. Meliksetov and L. P. Delyusin in *USSR–China in the Changing World* (Moscow: Novosti Press Agency Publishing House, 1989). For the Chinese perspective, see Wu Xiuquan. *Zai waijiaobu ba nian de jingli (1950.1–1958.10)* [Eight years in the foreign ministry (January 1950–October 1958)] (Beijing: Shijie zhishi chubanshe, 1983), chap. 1.

Chapter 5

1. My use of mass socialization agrees with Charles Hoffman's definition of "the active cultivation of 'socialist' behavior through widespread education and propaganda as well as changed working conditions and institutions." See Charles Hoffman, *The Chinese Worker* (Albany: State University of New York Press, 1974), p. 11.

2. Two good examples are *Gongren zhengzhi keben* [Political textbook for workers] (Shanghai: Xinhua shudian, 1950); and Xiao Ling and Xiao Yun, eds., *Xin gongren duben* [The new workers' textbook] (Shanghai: Xuesheng shudian faxing, 1949).

3. See *Gongren zhengzhi keben*, 1950.

4. Ibid., pp. 1–2.

5. Xiao Ling and Xiao Yun, eds., *Xin gongren duben*, p. 3.

6. *Gongren zhengzhi keben*, pp. 3–5.

7. Ibid., pp. 6–8.

8. This is a Soviet idea as reflected in the factory materials from the postwar period. Every Soviet citizen was expected to derive *personal satisfaction* from contributing to the public good through his or her work. See Chapter 2.

9. *Gongren zhengzhi keben*, pp. 9–11.

10. Ibid., pp. 12–13.

11. Ibid., pp. 16–17.

12. It was important for the communists to justify this deviation from the Soviet path of development, and so an entire lesson was devoted to this topic.

13. *Gongren zhengzhi keben*, pp. 18–19.

14. Li Shuxiang, *Wei shun chengren gongchandang shi gongren jiejide dang* [Recognize that the Communist party is the party of the working class] (Shandong: Shandong renmin chubanshe, 1952), pp. 14–15.

15. Ibid., pp. 18–23.

16. Ibid., pp. 24–26.

17. Ibid., pp. 27–29.

18. The new labor attitude includes working hard, respecting equipment, conserving raw materials, and keeping costs low and quality and quantity high. It also includes participation in socialist labor campaigns and labor emulation campaigns, as well as in the competitions to become labor heroes.

19. *Gongren zhengzhi keben*, pp. 30–31.

20. Ibid., pp. 34–35.

21. Ibid., pp. 41–42.

22. Ibid., pp. 1–2.

23. Hu Shiru and Liu Wenju, eds., *Gongye qiye shengchan zuzhi yu guanli* [Organization and management of industrial enterprise production] (Shanghai: Liyanhui tushe yongpinshe chuban, 1953), p. 23.

24. Ibid., pp. 219–21.

25. Ibid., p. 228.

26. Shi Liang, ed., *Gongchang guanli gailun* [An introduction to factory management] (Shanghai: Liyanhui tushe yongpinshe shuban, 1952), p. 36.

27. *Gongchandang yuande keben* [Textbook for Communist party members] (Dongan: Dongbeiju xuanchuanbu, 1947), p. 38.

28. Shi Liang, ed., *Gongchang guanli*, p. 36.

29. *Gongchandang yuande keben* [Textbook for Communist party members] (Hankou: Zhongnan renmin chubanshe, 1950), pp. 52–53.

30. *Gongchandang yuande keben*, 1947, p. 40.

31. *Gongchandang yuande keben*, 1950, pp. 54–55.

32. For an in-depth look at Party expansion campaigns during this period, see Fang Shu, *Campaign of Party-Expansion of the Chinese Communist Party in 1952* (Hong Kong: Union Research Institute, 1953).

33. Hu Shiru and Liu Wenju, eds., *Gongye qiye*, p. 221.

34. For the best discussion in English of one-man management, see Franz Schurmann, *Ideology and Organization in Communist China*, 2nd ed. (Berkeley and Los Angeles: University of California Press, 1968), pp. 253–84.

35. *Gongchandang yuande keben*, 1950, pp. 57–58.

36. See, for instance, F. V. Konstantinov, *Rol' sotsialisticheskogo soznaniya v razvitii sovetskogo obshchestva* [The role of socialist consciousness in the development of Soviet society] (Moscow: Pravda, 1948); his *O dvizhushchikh silakh razvitiya sotsialisticheskogo obshchestva* [On the driving force of the development of socialist society] (Moscow: Pravda, 1948); and his *Rol' peredovykh idei v obshchestvennom razvitii* [The role of advanced ideas in the development of society] (Moscow: Pravda, 1947).

37. See Konstantinov's chapter, "The Conditions for Molding the Masses' Socialist Consciousness," *Rol' sotsialisticheskogo soznaniya v razvitii*, pp. 16–22.

38. Ibid., p. 18.

39. *Xuanchuanyuan gongzuo shouce* [Handbook of propagandists' work] (Shanghai: Huadong renmin chubanshe, 1951); *Xuanchuan gongzuo wenyi* [Collected propaganda works] (Hankou: Zhongnan renmin chubanshe, 1951); Jiang Shui, *Chusede xuanchuanyuan* [Outstanding propagandists] (Beijing: Gongren chubanshe, 1951); *Zenyang gonggu gongchang zhongde xuanchuanwang* [How to strengthen the factory propaganda network] (Shanghai: Huadong renmin chubanshe, 1951); *Gongchang zhongde shishi xuanchuan jiaowu* [Teaching current events propaganda in the factory] (Shanghai: Laodong chubanshe, 1951); *Shengchan zhongde xuanchuan guli* [Propaganda and encouragement in production] (n.p.: 1950?).

40. *Gongchang wenyi* [Factory art and literature] 1 (December 1949) (Tangshan: Tangshanshi zong gonghui jiaoyubu, 1949); *Gongren shenghuo* [Workers' life-style], vol. 1, no. 4 (Subei: Gongren shenghuoshe, 1950); *Gongren wenyi* [Workers' art and literature], no. 6 (1950).

41. The Party was advised to emphasize the link between patriotism and production, just as the CPSU had been portrayed as having accomplished in the postwar literature. Party members were urged to organize "patriotic pledges" in socialist competitions and emulation campaigns. See *Zenyang gonggu gongchang zhongde xuanchuanwang*, p. 7.

42. See, for instance, Wu Qingyou, *Sulian gongye guanli* [Soviet enter-

prise management] (Shanghai: Zhonghua shuju yinxing, 1950), pp. 56–65. For a comprehensive review of the Soviet campaigns themselves, see V. B. Tel'pukhovskii, ed., *Rabochii klass SSSR v gody uprocheniya i razvitiya sotsial-isticheskogo obshchestva 1945–1960 gg.* [The working class of the USSR during the years of consolidation and development of socialist society, 1945–1960], vol. 4 (Moscow: Nauka, 1987).

43. *Zenyang gonggu gongchang zhongde xuanchuanwang,* p. 5.

44. Ibid., pp. 8–10.

45. Ibid., pp. 11–13.

46. There are several good English-language sources on China's labor unions, such as Jeanne L. Wilson, "Trade Unions in Communist States; the People's Republic of China," Wheaton College, unpublished manuscript, 1988; Lee Lai To, *Trade Unions in China, 1949 to the Present* (Singapore: Singapore University Press, 1986); Paul E. Harper, "Political Roles of Trade Unions in Communist China" (Ph.D. diss., University of Michigan, 1969). There is a well-developed Soviet literature on trade unions, including A. P. Davydov, *Profsoyuzy KNR, 1953–1958 gg.* [Trade unions in the PRC, 1953–1958] (Moscow: Nauka, 1978); A. P. Davydov, *Profsoyuzy Kitaya, istoriya i sovremennost'* [Trade unions of China, yesterday and today] (Moscow: Profizdat, 1981); B. G. Gel'bras, *Rabochii klass Kitaya (1949–1974 gg.)* [The working class of China, 1949–1974] (Moscow: Nauka, 1978).

47. For detailed instructions on organizing trade union committees at every level and the tasks of each committee, see *Gonghui zuzhi gongzuo youguan wenjian* [Documents on trade union organizational work] (Shanghai: Laodong chubanshe, 1951).

48. Hu Shiru and Liu Wenju, eds., *Gongye qiye,* p. 221.

49. Wu Shushen, "A Discussion on Deliberating the Selection of the Workshop Manager," *Zhongguo gongye* 1 (October 1949): 24–25.

50. Shi Liang, ed., *Gongchang guanli,* pp. 235–39.

51. See also *Laodong baoxian wenti* [Labor insurance questions], pt. 1 (Beijing: Gongren chubanshe, 1951).

52. *Gongren wenhua keben* [Culture textbook for workers], vol. 2 (Shanghai: Lianhe chubanshe, 1950).

53. *Gongren keben* [Workers' textbook], vols. 1–4 (Shanghai: Laodong chubanshe, 1950).

54. *Gongren wenhua keben,* vol. 2, 1950, p. 46.

55. See, for instance, Bai Yuan and Bai Shi, trans. and eds., "Problems of Trade Union Work in the Enterprise," in *Xuexi Sulian qiye gongzuo jingyan* [We study the Soviet experience in enterprise work] (Beijing: Dazhong shudian chuban, 1950); D. Pichaluofu, "How the Polish Trade Unions Struggle to Improve Industry," *Zhongguo gongye* [Chinese industry] 2 (September 1950):3; Zheng Hongshu, "The Relationship Between Soviet Trade Unions and Economic Development," *Zhongguo gongye* [Chinese industry] 1 (December 1949):27–32; Zhu Cishou, "How Does the Soviet Union Increase Labor Productivity in Industry?" *Zhongguo gongye* [Chinese industry] 2 (May 1950):3–9.

56. Feng Tian, *Gongxiao yiyueji* [A monthly diary of work efficiency] (Tianjin: Duzhe shudian, 1950).

57. See, for instance, Song Zhengquan, "Research on Increasing Labor Productivity," *Zhongguo gongye* [Chinese industry] 2 (May 1950):19–23.

58. Gao Guang, *Tan chuangzao xingde laodong* [On the creativity of labor] (Shanghai: Renmin chubanshe, 1956.)

59. Hu Shiru and Liu Wenju, eds., *Gongye qiye*, p. 227.

60. Ibid.

61. See A Ying, *Gongchang wenyu gongzuo de lilin yu shijian* [Theory and practice of factory leisure activities work] (Beijing: Shenghuo dushu xinzhi sanlan shudian faxing, 1950).

62. *Xiang gongchan zhuyi quanjinde Sulian qingnian* [Soviet youth forge ahead under Communism] (Hankou: Zhongnan qingnian chushe chuban, 1952).

63. The 1939 campaign entailed a "basic rectification methodology" of intensive education, small-group study, criticism and self-criticism, and thought reform, which, it could be argued, had its origins in Soviet practice. See Mark Selden, *The Yenan Way in Revolutionary China* (Cambridge, MA: Harvard University Press, 1971), pp. 188–200.

Chapter 6

1. As defined by the CCP, mass organizations included the Chinese Communist Party, the Labor Union, the Democratic Youth Group, the Peasants' Associations, the Democratic Womens' Federation, the Democratic Students' Federation, and others. This book concentrates only on the first three, which were the most important organizations in the factory.

2. Franz Schurmann, *Ideology and Organization in Communist China*, 2nd ed. (Berkeley and Los Angeles: University of California Press, 1968), p. 314. On "control commissions" in Canton, see Ezra Vogel, *Canton Under Communism: Programs and Politics in a Provincial Capital, 1949–1968* (New York: Harper & Row, 1969), p. 50.

3. In 1949/1950, the CCP still was struggling to eliminate the old gang boss and secret society systems. Many factories received a PLA (People's Liberation Army) contingent for "economic protection work" to guard against "sabotage and wrecking." In others, the Public Security Bureau held training sessions for workers so that they could organize their own security groups and "factory protection corps." The Chinese press discussed this rather openly, as seen in *Survey of the China Mainland Press*, November 19–20, 1950, pp. 14–15, and *Survey of the China Mainland Press*, January 7–8, 1951, p. 8.

4. *Hongqi*, November 1, 1959, as cited in Charles P. Cell, *Revolution at Work: Mobilization Campaigns in China* (New York: Academic Press, 1977), p. 7.

5. For an excellent discussion of this process in Tianjin (Tientsin), see Kenneth G. Lieberthal, *Revolution and Tradition in Tientsin, 1949–1952* (Stanford, CA: Stanford University Press, 1980), pp. 34–37.

6. D. Eleanor Westney, *Imitation and Innovation: The Transfer of Western Organizational Patterns to Meiji Japan* (Cambridge: Cambridge University Press, 1987).

7. Lieberthal, *Revolution and Tradition*, p. 45. See also William Brugger's exhaustive treatment in *Democracy and Organisation in the Chinese Industrial Enterprise (1948–1953)* (Cambridge: Cambridge University Press, 1976).

8. See Vogel, *Canton Under Communism*, pp. 76–77.

9. See A. Doak Barnett, *Communist China: The Early Years 1949–55* (New York: Praeger, 1964), pp. 34–35.

10. Shi Liang, ed., *Gongchang guanli gailun* [An introduction to factory management] (Shanghai: Liyanhui tushe yongpinshe chuban, 1952), pp. 34–36.

11. See, for instance, the *Pravda* editorial from May 29, 1950 ("Communists Must Be Trained Through Practical Work"), which was translated into Chinese by Bai Yuan and Bai Shi, trans. and eds., "Problems of the Party–Mass Relationship in the Enterprise," in *Xuexi Sulian qiye gongzuo jingyan* [We study the Soviet experience in enterprise work] (Beijing: Dazhong shudian chuban, 1950), pp. 44–48. See also a *Pravda* article from March 6, 1948 ("On the Party Committee's Work"), which was translated into Chinese by Jie Fangshe, ed., *Sulian gongchandangde jianshe wenti* [Problems of Soviet Communist party construction] (Beijing: Xinhua shudian, 1949), pp. 97–105.

12. D. Goginava, *Partiinii kontrol' na predpriyatii* [Party control in the enterprise] (Moscow: Gospolitizdat, 1949), pp. 11–15.

13. Ibid., p. 120.

14. Ibid., p. 131.

15. Ibid., p. 132.

16. See Hu Shiru and Liu Wenju, eds., *Gongye qiye shengchang zuzhi yu guanli* [Organization and management of industrial enterprises and factories] (Shanghai: Liyanhui tushe yongpinshe chuban, 1953), p. 221.

17. Shi Liang, ed., *Gongchang guanli*, p. 40.

18. Chai Fu, "Give Free Rein to the Party's Great Power to Lead the Masses to Advance," *Shanxi ribao*, October 2, 1950, p. 3.

19. See, for instance, *Zhongguo gongye* [Chinese industry] 2 (September 1950):n.p.

20. See, for example, the Conference for Worker, Peasant, Soldier Model Workers in October in Beijing, in *Shandong ribao*, October 5, 1950, p. 3.

21. See Brugger, *Democracy and Organisation*, pp. 164–65, for a good summary of Ma's career.

22. See, for instance, *Xianjin shengchan xiaozu* [Small groups for advanced production] (Beijing: Gongren chubanshe, 1951); and *Ma Hengchang xiaozu jingsai yundong* [The Ma Hengchang small group competition movement] (Beijing: Gongren chubanshe, 1951).

23. See, for instance, Zhu Cishou, "How Does the Soviet Union Increase Labor Productivity in Industry?" *Zhongguo gongye* 2 (1950):3–9; Zheng Hongshu, "Socialist Competition and the Stakhanov Movement," *Zhongguo gongye* 1 (January 1950):27–36.

24. Again, as seen in the Soviet literature, the Chinese communists believed that under capitalism, new management techniques are always secret but that under socialism, the work of each worker, and of each enterprise, is not only society's but also the nation's business.

25. Hu Shiru and Liu Wenju, eds., *Gongye qiye*, pp. 160–61.

26. See Lee Lai To, *Trade Unions in China, 1949 to the Present* (Singapore: Singapore University Press, 1986), for a summary of labor union activities in practice.

27. *Shandong ribao*, October 2, 1950, pp. 3–4.

28. This campaign began on October 13, 1950, when the famous labor hero Chao Kuoyu and other workers at Plant No. 3 of the Mukden Machine Tool Factory issued a challenge to all other Manchurian workers for an emulation drive that would "strengthen the fatherland, defend world peace and oppose the American aggressors." Translated in New China News Agency, *Daily News Release,* November 9, 1950, pp. 72–73.

29. Ibid., November 4, 1950, p. 36.

30. *Qingniantuan gongkuang xiaozu gongzuo jingyan* [The experience of youth small groups in factories and mines] (Beijing: Qingnian chubanshe, 1951), pp. 2–3.

31. Ong Shao-er, *Labor Problems in Communist China (to February 1953),* Research Memorandum no. 42 (Lackland Air Force Base, TX: U.S. Air Force Personnel and Training Research Center, 1955).

32. Gao Guang, *Tan chuangzao xingde laodong* [On the creativity of labor] (Shanghai: Renmin chubanshe, 1956).

33. Hu Shiru and Liu Wenju, eds., *Gongye qiye,* p. 227.

34. See A Ying, *Gongchang wenyu gongzuo de lilun yu shijian* [Theory and practice of factory leisure activities work] (Beijing: Shenghuo dushu xinzhi sanlan shudian faxing, 1950).

35. Lieberthal, *Revolution and Tradition,* pp. 187–88.

36. Zhu Pu, "The Great New Records Movement," *Zhongguo gongye* [Chinese industry] 1 (December 1950): 3–16.

37. For a good review of both the building and the rectification of the Party during this period, see Harry Harding, *Organizing China: The Problem of Bureaucracy, 1949–1976* (Stanford, CA: Stanford University Press, 1981), pp. 34–47.

38. See Vogel, *Canton Under Communism,* p. 63.

39. Stephen Andors, ed., *Workers and Workplaces in Revolutionary China* (White Plains, NY: M. E. Sharpe, Inc., 1977), p. 92.

40. See William Brugger, *China: Liberation and Transformation 1942–1962* (London: Croom Helm, 1981), pp. 73–74.

41. Barnett, *Communist China,* p. 47.

42. New China News Agency, *Daily News Release,* November 9, 1950, pp. 72–73.

43. Liu Hsin-hua, "Patriotic Emulation Sweeps Industry," *People's China,* June 1, 1951, p. 12.

44. New China News Agency, *Daily News Release,* December 13, 1950, p. 102.

45. "Consolidate Our Great Motherland Under the Banner of Patriotism." *Renmin ribao, Survey of the China Mainland Press,* January 1–3, 1951.

46. See the discussion about the development of the movement in a factory for the purposes of teaching young workers about patriotism, in *Qingniantuan gongkuang,* pp. 36–38.

47. See *Xuanchuanyuan shouce* [A manual for propagandists] (Dongbei: Xinhua shudian, 1951), various issues. In no. 21 (April), for instance, is a page called "Heibanbao" [Blackboard newspaper], which is just a written message to be copied exactly from the book onto a blackboard. The propaganda concerned Chinese war losses in the war against the imperialist Americans in Korea.

48. *Qingniantuan gongkuang*, p. 17.

49. Liu Hsin-hua, "Patriotic Emulation," p. 12.

50. William Brugger, *Democracy and Organisation*, pp. 100–4; A. P. Davydov, *Profsoyuzy KNR* [Labor unions in the PRC] (Moscow: Nauka, 1978); Paul Harper, "Political Roles of Trade Unions in Communist China" (Ph.D. diss., University of Michigan, 1969); Paul Harper, "The Party and the Unions in Communist China," *China Quarterly* 37 (January–March 1969):84–119; Ong Shao-er, *Labor Problems in Communist China*; Jeanne L. Wilson, "Trade Unions in Communist States: The People's Republic of China," Wheaton College, 1988, unpublished manuscript.

51. See Lee Lai To, *Trade Unions in China*, p. 38.

52. "Is It Possible That Our Small Group Still Wastes?" *Gongnong huabao* [Worker and peasant pictorial], no. 15 (Shanghai: Huadong renmin chubanshe, 1951).

53. See Jonathan D. Spence, *The Search for Modern China* (New York: Norton, 1990), p. 536; Brugger, *China*, pp. 80–83.

54. Brugger, *China*, p. 82.

55. Quoted in Barnett, *Communist China*, p. 135.

56. Ibid., pp. 135–57.

57. Mark Selden, *The Yenan Way in Revolutionary China* (Cambridge, MA: Harvard University Press, 1971), p. 134.

58. See discussion in Maurice Meisner, *Mao's China: A History of the People's Republic* (New York: Free Press, 1977), pp. 76–82.

Chapter 7

1. *Gongren zhengzhi keben* [Political textbook for workers] (Shanghai: Xinhua shudian, 1950), p. 1.

2. N. Fedorenko, "The Stalin–Mao Summit," *Far Eastern Affairs* 2 (1989): 139.

3. Lynn T. White III has argued, and I think successfully, that the early emphasis on class divisions and other CCP policies set the stage for other, more harmful, mass movements like the Cultural Revolution. See his *Politics of Chaos* (Princeton, NJ: Princeton University Press, 1989).

Bibliography

Ai Mu et al. *Zenyang lingdao gongchang* [How to manage a factory]. Dalian: Dalian dazhong shudian yinxing, 1947.

Aird, John S. "Recent Demographic Data from China: Problems and Prospects." In Joint Economic Committee, *China Under the Four Modernizations*. Pt. 1, pp. 171–223. Washington, DC: U.S. Government Printing Office, 1982.

Akatova, T. N. *Rabochee dvizheniye v gomin'danovskom Kitae 1927–1937 gg.* [The workers' movement in guomindang China, 1927–1937]. Moscow: Nauka, 1983.

Alakelian, A. "Socialist Enterprise Management." Trans. Hu Shiru. *Zhongguo gongye* [Chinese industry] 2 (July 1950): 5–11.

Andors, Stephen. *China's Industrial Revolution*. New York: Pantheon Books, 1977.

——, ed. *Workers and Workplaces in Revolutionary China*. The China Book Project, Translation and Commentary. White Plains, NY: M. E. Sharpe, 1977.

Arakelian, A. *Industrial Management in the USSR*. Trans. Ellsworth L. Raymond. Washington, DC: Public Affairs Press, 1950.

Astafyev, G. V. *China's Economic Problems*. Bombay: People's Publishing House, 1950.

A Ying. *Gongchang wenyu gongzuo de lilun yu shijian* [Theory and practice of factory leisure activities work]. Beijing: Shenghuo dushu xinzhi sanlan shudian faxing, 1950.

Bai Yuan and Bai Shi, trans. and eds. "Problems of Labor Union Work in the Enterprise." In *Xuexi Sulian qiye gongzuo jingyan* [We study the Soviet experience in enterprise work]. Beijing: Dazhong shudian chuban, 1950.

———, trans. and eds. "Problems of the Mass–Party Relationship in the Enterprise." In *Xuexi Sulian qiye gongzuo jingyan* [We study the Soviet experience in enterprise work]. Beijing: Dazhong shudian chuban, 1950.

Barnett, A. Doak. *China on the Eve of Communist Takeover*. 2nd ed. Boulder, CO: Westview Press, 1985.

———. *Communist China: The Early Years 1949–55*. New York: Praeger, 1964.

Berliner, Joseph S. *Factory and Manager in the USSR*. Cambridge, MA: Harvard University Press, 1957.

———. "Managerial Incentives and Decision-making: A Comparison of the United States and the Soviet Union." In Joseph S. Berliner, *Soviet Industry from Stalin to Gorbachev: Essays on Management and Innovation*. Ithaca, NY: Cornell University Press, 1988.

Bialer, Seweryn. *Stalin's Successors: Leadership, Stability, and Change in the Soviet Union*. Cambridge: Cambridge University Press, 1980.

Bianco, Lucian. *Origins of the Chinese Revolution, 1915–1949*. Trans. Muriel Bell. Stanford, CA: Stanford University Press, 1971.

Bienstock, Gregory, Solomon M. Schwarz, and Aaron Yugow. *Management in Russian Industry and Agriculture*. Ithaca, NY: Cornell University Press, 1948.

Boichenko, S. N. "The Drawing in of Youths into the Ranks of the Working Class During the War and in the First Postwar Years." In *Problemy vosstanovleniya i dal'neishego razvitiya narodnogo khozyaistva SSSR* [The problems of reconstruction and further development of the USSR national economy]. Moscow: Akademiya obshchestvennykh nauk pri TsK KPSS, 1978.

Borisov, O. B., and B. T. Koloskov. *Sovetsko–Kitaiskie otnosheniya, 1945–1980* [Soviet–Chinese relations, 1945–1980]. 3rd ed. Moscow: Mysl', 1980.

Bo Yibo. *Ruogan zhongde juece yu shijian de huigu* [A review of some very important policies and events]. Vol. 1, 1949-1956. Beijing: Zhonggong zhongyang dangxiao chubanshe, 1991.

Brugger, William. *China: Liberation and Transformation 1942–1962*. London: Croom Helm, 1981.

———. *Democracy and Organisation in the Chinese Industrial Enterprise (1948–1953)*. Cambridge: Cambridge University Press, 1976.

Cell, Charles P. *Revolution at Work: Mobilization Campaigns in China*. New York: Academic Press, 1977.

Central Heavy Industrial Ministry's Personnel Office, Labor and Wages Department, ed. and trans. *Gangtie gongye de laodong zuzhi* [Labor organizations in the iron and steel industry]. Beijing: Kexue jishu chubanshe, 1952.

Chai Fu. "Give Free Rein to the Party's Great Power to Lead the Masses to Advance." *Shanxi ribao*, October 2, 1950, p. 3.

Chen, Nai-Ruenn, and Walter Galenson. *The Chinese Economy Under Communism*. Chicago: Aldine, 1969.

Chen Yongwen. *Gongchang guanli minzhuhua wenti jianghua* [Discussion of problems of factory management democratization]. Beijing: Gongren chubanshe yinxing, 1950.

Cheng, Chu-Yuan. *Communist China's Economy, 1949–1962.* West Orange, NJ: Seton Hall University Press, 1963.

Chernyak, N. *Partiinaya organizatsiya i sotsialisticheskoe sorevnovanie* [The party organization and socialist competition]. Moscow: Moskovskii rabochii, 1948.

Chesneaux, Jean. *The Chinese Labor Movement, 1919–1927.* Trans. H. M. Wright. Stanford, CA: Stanford University Press, 1968.

Current Background. Hong Kong: American Counsel General, 1950–1953.

Davydov, A. P. *Profsoyuzy Kitaya: istoriya i sovremennost'* [Labor unions of China: Yesterday and today]. Moscow: Profizdat, 1981.

———. *Profsoyuzy KNR, 1953–1958 gg.* [Labor unions in the PRC, 1953–1958]. Moscow: Nauka, 1978.

Delyusin, L. P. *Rabochee dvizheniye v Kitae, nankinskii gomin'dan i rabochii vopros (1927–1931)* [The workers' movement in China, the Nanjing Guomindang and the labor question (1927–1931)]. Moscow: Nauka, 1982.

Deng Fadeng. *Lun gongying gongchang* [On the state-owned factory]. Dongbei: Dongbei shudian, 1946.

Ding'e guanli [Management of plan quotas]. Beijing: Renmin chubanshe, 1951.

Dirlik, Arlif. *The Origins of Chinese Communism.* New York: Oxford University Press, 1989.

Dongbei gongying qiyede jingying yu jingli [Economy and management of the northeast's state-owned enterprises]. Beijing: Xinhua shudian faxing, 1950.

Ellison, Herbert J., ed. *The Sino-Soviet Conflict: A Global Perspective.* Seattle: University of Washington Press, 1982.

Emerson, John Philip. "Employment in Mainland China: Problems and Prospects." In Joint Economic Committee, *An Economic Profile of Mainland China.* Vol. 2, pp. 403–69. Washington, DC: U.S. Government Printing Office, 1967.

Fakiolis, R. "Problems of Labour Mobility in the USSR." *Soviet Studies* 14 (July 1962): 17.

Fang Shu. *Campaign of Party-Expansion of the Chinese Communist Party in 1952.* Hong Kong: Union Research Institute, 1954.

FBIS (Foreign Broadcast Information Bureau). Translations of the Soviet press, various years.

Fedorenko, N. "The Stalin–Mao Summit in Moscow." *Far Eastern Affairs* 2 (1989): 134–48.

Feng Tian. *Gongxiao yiyueji* [A monthly diary of work efficiency]. Tianjin: Duzhe shudian, 1950.

Filatov, L. V. *Ekonomicheskaya otsenka nauchno-tekhnicheskoi pomoshchi Sovetsogo Soyuza Kitayu 1949–1966* [An economic evaluation of scientific and technical assistance of the Soviet Union to China, 1949–1966]. Moscow: Nauka, 1980.

Fitzpatrick, Sheila. "Postwar Soviet Society: The 'Return to Normalcy', 1945–1953." In *The Impact of World War II on the Soviet Union*. Ed. Susan J. Linz, pp. 129–56. Totowa, NJ: Rowman & Allanheld, 1985.

Foreign Relations of the United States. Vol. 3: *China: Internal and Foreign Affairs, 1940–1949*. Washington, DC: U.S. Government Printing Office, 1978.

Gao Guang. *Tan chuangzao xingde laodong* [On the creativity of labor]. Shanghai: Renmin chubanshe, 1956.

Gel'bras, V. G. *Maoizm i rabochii klass Kitaya* [Maoism and China's working class]. Moscow: Profizdat, 1972.

———, ed. *Rabochii klass Kitaya (1949–1974 gg.)* [The working class of China (1949–1974). Moscow: Nauka, 1978.

———. *Sotsial'no-politicheskaya struktura KNR 50–60e gody* [Social and political structure of the PRC in the 1950s and 1960s]. Moscow: Nauka, 1980.

Gliksman, Jerzy. *Postwar Trends in Soviet Labor Policy*. RAND Research Memorandum no. P-754. Santa Monica, CA: RAND Corporation, 1955.

——— et al. *The Control of Industrial Labor in the Soviet Union*. RAND Research Memorandum no. 2494. Santa Monica, CA: RAND Corporation, 1960.

Goginava, D. *Partiinii kontrol' na predpriyatii* [Party control in the enterprise]. Moscow: Gospolitizdat, 1949.

Gongchandang yuande keben [Textbook for Communist party members]. Dongan: Dongbeiju xuanchuanbu, 1947.

Gongchandang yuande keben [Textbook for Communist party members]. Hankou: Zhongnan renmin chubanshe, 1950.

Gongchang wenyi [Factory art and literature] 1 (December 1949). Tangshan: Tangshanshi zong gonghui jiaoyubu, 1949.

Gongchang zhongde shishi xuanchuan jiaowu [Teaching current events propaganda in the factory]. Shanghai: Laodong chubanshe, 1951.

Gonghui zuzhi gongzuo youguan wenjian [Documents on labor union organizational work]. Shanghai: Laodong chubanshe, 1951.

Gong nong huabao [Worker and peasant picture newspaper]. Shanghai: Huadong renmin chubanshe, 1951.

Gongren keben [Workers' textbook]. Vols. 1–4. Shanghai: Laodong chubanshe, 1950.

Gongren shenghuo [Workers' life-style]. Vol. 1, no. 4. Subei: Gongren shenghuoshe, 1950.

Gongren wenhua keben [Culture textbook for workers]. Vols. 1–4. Shanghai: Lianhe chubanshe, 1950.

Gongren wenyi [Workers' art and literature] 6 (1950).

Gongren zhengzhi keben [Political textbook for workers]. Shanghai: Xinhua shudian, 1950.

Gongyun wenti yibaige [One hundred questions on the workers' movement]. Pt. 1. Beijing: Gongren chubanshe yinxing, 1950.

Granick, David. *Management of the Industrial Firm in the USSR: A Study in Soviet Economic Planning.* New York: Columbia University Press, 1954.

———. *Managerial Comparisons of Four Developed Countries: France, Britain, United States and Russia.* Cambridge, MA: MIT Press, 1972.

———. *The Red Executive: A Study of the Organization Man in Russian Industry.* Garden City, NY: Doubleday, 1961.

Guan Shuixin. "Three Years of Economic Construction in the Northeast." *Zhongguo gongye* [Chinese industry] 1 (November 1950): 18–22.

Haimson, Leopold. "Decision-making and Communications in Soviet Industry." In *Studies in Soviet Communication.* Vol. 2. Cambridge, MA: MIT Center for International Studies, 1952.

Harding, Harry. *Organizing China: The Problem of Bureaucracy, 1949–1976.* Stanford, CA: Stanford University Press, 1981.

Harper, Paul E. "The Party and the Unions in Communist China." *China Quarterly* 37 (January–March 1969): 84–119.

———. "Political Roles of Trade Unions in Communist China." Ph.D. Diss., University of Michigan, 1969.

Henley, John S., and Nyaw Mee-Kau. "The Development of Work Incentives in Chinese Industrial Enterprises—Material Versus Non-Material Incentives." In *Management Reforms in China.* Ed. M. Warner, pp. 127–48. London: Frances Pinter.

Hershatter, Gail. *The Workers of Tianjin, 1900–1949.* Stanford, CA: Stanford University Press, 1986.

Hoffman, Charles. *The Chinese Worker.* Albany: State University of New York Press, 1974.

Honig, Emily. *Sisters and Strangers: Women in the Shanghai Cotton Mills, 1919–1949.* Stanford, CA: Stanford University Press, 1986.

Hosking, Geoffrey. *The First Socialist Society.* Cambridge, MA: Harvard University Press, 1985.

Hough, Jerry. *The Soviet Prefects.* Cambridge, MA: Harvard University Press, 1969.

Hough, Jerry F., and Merle Fainsod. *How the Soviet Union Is Governed.* Cambridge, MA: Harvard University Press, 1979.

Hu Lintai, ed. *Sui xin gongchang guanli fa* [The newest factory management methods]. Tianjin: Yishi shudian, 1951.

Hu Shiru and Liu Wenju, eds. *Gongye qiye shengchang zuzhi yu guanli* [Organization and management of industrial enterprises and factories]. Shanghai: Liyanhui tushe yongpinshe chuban, 1953.

"Is It Possible That Our Small Group Still Wastes?" *Gongnong huabao* [Worker and peasant pictorial], no. 15. Shanghai: Huadong renmin chubanshe, 1951.

Istoriya sotsialisticheskogo sorevnovaniya v SSSR [The history of socialist competition in the USSR]. Moscow: Profizdat, 1980.

Jasny, Naum. *Soviet Industrialization 1928–1952.* Chicago: University of Chicago Press, 1961.

Jenner, W. J. F. *The Tyranny of History: The Roots of China's Crisis.* London: Lane, 1992.

Jiang Shui. *Chusede xuanchuanyuan* [Outstanding propagandists]. Beijing: Gongren chubanshe, 1951.

Jianguo yilai Mao Zedong wengao [Mao Zedong communications from the founding of the PRC]. Vol. 1, September 1949–December 1950. Beijing: Zhongyang wenxian chushe, 1990.

Jie Fangshe, ed. *Sulian gongchandangde jianshe wenti* [Problems of Soviet Communist Party construction]. Beijing: Xinhua shudian, 1949.

Kaplan, Cynthia S. "The Impact of World War II on the Party." In *The Impact of World War II on the Soviet Union*, ed. Susan J. Linz, pp. 157–88. Totowa, NJ: Rowman & Allanheld, 1985.

Kartunova, A. I. *Politika kompartii Kitaya v rabochem voprose nakanune revolyutsii 1925–1927* [The policies of the Communist party of China in the worker's question on the eve of the revolution, 1925–1927]. Moscow: Nauka, 1983.

Khlusov, M. I., ed. *Promyshlennost' i rabochii klass SSSR, 1946–1950: dokumenty i materialy* [Industry and the working class in the USSR, 1946-1950: Documents and materials]. Moscow: Nauka, 1989.

———. *Razvitie sovetskoi industrii 1946–1958* [The development of Soviet industry, 1946–1958]. Moscow: Nauka, 1977.

Khor'kov, V. I. *Nankinskii gomin'dan i rabochii vopros, 1927–1932* [The Nanjing Guomindang and the worker question, 1927–1932]. Moscow: Nauka, 1977.

Khrushchev, N. S. *Khrushchev Remembers*. Boston: Little Brown, 1970.

Klochko, M. A. *Soviet Scientist in Red China*. Trans. Andrew MacAndrew. New York: Praeger, 1964.

Kommunisticheskaya partiya sovetskogo soyuza v rezolyutsiyakh i resheniyakh s"ezdov, konferentsiy i plenumov TsK [The Communist party of the Soviet Union in resolutions and decisions of congresses, conferences and plenums of the Central Committee]. Vol. 8, 1946–1955. Moscow: Izdatel'stvo politicheskoi literatury 1985.

Konstantinov, F. V. *O dvizhushchikh silakh razvitiya sotsialisticheskogo obshchestva* [On the driving force of the development of socialist society]. Moscow: Pravda, 1948.

———. *Rol' peredovykh idei v obshchestvennom razvitii* [The role of advanced ideas in the development of society]. Moscow: Pravda, 1947.

———. *Rol' sotsialisticheskogo soznaniya v razvitii sovetskogo obshchestva* [The role of socialist consciousness in the development of Soviet society]. Moscow: Pravda, 1948.

Kraus, Willy. *Economic Development and Social Change in the People's Republic of China*. Trans. E. M. Holz. New York: Springer-Verlag, 1982.

Kremnyeva, O. *Opyt politicheskoi agitatsii na predpriyatii* [The experience of political agitation in the enterprise]. Moscow: Gospolitizdat, 1948.

Kuromiya, Hiroaki. *Stalin's Industrial Revolution: Politics and Workers, 1928–1932*. Cambridge: Cambridge University Press, 1988.

Laodong bao [Workers' Newspaper], 1949–1953.

Laodong baoxian wenti [Labor insurance questions]. Pt. 1. Beijing: Gongren chubanshe, 1951.

Lebedeva, N.B. *Partiinoe rukovodstvo sotsialisticheskim sorevnovaniem: istoriya i sovremennost'* [Party leadership of socialist competition: history and contemporaneity]. Leningrad: Lenizdat, 1979.

Lee Lai To. *Trade Unions in China, 1949 to the Present*. Singapore: Singapore University Press, 1986.

Leningradskaya Pravda, 1946–1949.

Leskov, A. "Party Groups in the Enterprises." *Pravda*, June 17, 1949, p. 2.

Levine, Steven I. *Anvil of Victory: The Communist Revolution in Manchuria, 1945–1948*. New York: Columbia University Press, 1987.

Lieberthal, Kenneth G. *Revolution and Tradition in Tientsin, 1949–1952*. Stanford, CA: Stanford University Press, 1980.

Lieu, D. K. *China's Economic Stabilization and Reconstruction*. New Brunswick, NJ: Rutgers University Press, 1948.

Li Mingsan. "Important Topics Promotive of the Study of the History of the CCP." *Qiushi* 11 (1988): 43–44. Trans. Foreign Broadcast Information Service, February 3, 1989, pp. 16–18.

Li Shuxiang. *Wei shun chengren gongchandang shi gongren jiejide dang* [Recognize that the Communist Party is the Party of the working class]. Shandong: Shandong renmin chubanshe, 1952.

Liu Hsin-hua. "Patriotic Emulation Sweeps Industry." *People's China*, June 1, 1951, p. 12.

Lozovskii, A. *Rabochii Kitai v 1927 godu: sbornik statei* [Laboring China in 1927: Handbook of articles]. Moscow: Profintern, 1928.

Ma Hengchang xiaozu jingsai yundong [The Ma Hengchang small-group competition movement]. Beijing: Gongren chubanshe, 1951.

Malenkov, G. M. *O zadachakh partiinykh organizatsii v oblasti promyshlennosti i transporta* [On the tasks of party organizations in the areas of industry and transport]. Moscow: Gospolitizdat, 1941.

Mao Tse-tung. *A Critique of Soviet Economics*. Trans. Moss Roberts. New York: Monthly Review Press, 1977.

———. *Selected Works of Mao Tse-tung*. Vol. 5. Peking: Foreign Languages Press, 1977.

Maslova, N. S. *Proizvoditel'nost' truda v promyshlennosti SSSR* [Labor productivity in industry in the USSR]. Moscow: Gosudarstvennoe izdatel'stvo politicheskoi literatury, 1949.

McMillan, Charles J. "The Structure of Work Organization Across Societies." *Academy of Management Journal* 16 (1973): 555–69.

McNeal, Robert H. *Stalin: Man and Ruler*. London: Macmillan, 1988.

Medvedev, Roy A. *Let History Judge*. Trans. Colleen Taylor. New York: Vintage Books, 1971.

Meisner, Maurice. *Mao's China: A History of the People's Republic*. New York: Free Press, 1977.

Merzalov, Wladimir S., ed. *Biographic Dictionary of the USSR*. Munich: Institute for the Study of the USSR, 1958. English ed., New York: Scarecrow Press, 1958.

Meyer, John, and W. Richard Scott, eds. *Organizational Environments*. Beverly Hills, CA: Sage, 1983.

Mogilenko, P., and V. Zasetskii, *Organizatsiya raboty proizvodsvennykh soveshchanii* [Organizational work of the production conference]. Moscow: Profizdat, 1950.

Molodtsova, L. I. *Osobennosti formirovaniya promyshlennoi sistemy KNR, 1949–1985* [The peculiarities of the formation of the industrial system of the PRC, 1949–1985]. Moscow: Nauka, 1988.

Moore, Barrington, Jr. *Social Origins of Dictatorship and Democracy: Lord and Peasant in the Making of the Modern World*. Boston: Beacon Press, 1966.

"Mosike maozhi gongchang canguanji" [Notes from a visit to a Moscow knitting factory"]. *Gongren ribao* [Worker's Daily], December 2, 1949, p. 5.

Murachev, V., and M. Koshonina. *Naglyadnaya agitatsiya na predpriyatii* [Visual agitation at the enterprise]. Moscow: Gospolitizdat, 1953.

Muromtseva, Z. A. *Problemy industrializatsii Kitaiskoi narodnoi respubliki* [Problems of industrialization in the Chinese People's Republic]. Moscow: Nauka, 1971.

Narodnoe khozyaistvo SSSR 1922–1972, Yubileinii statisticheskii yezhegodnik [The national economy of the USSR, 1922–1972, jubilee statistical yearbook]. Moscow: Statistika, 1972

Narodnoe khozyaistvo SSSR; statisticheskii sbornik [The national economy of the USSR; statistical handbook]. Moscow: Gosudarstvennoe statisticheskoe izdatel'stvo, 1956.

Narodnoe khozyaistvo v 1958 g (The national economy in 1958). Moscow: Gosudarstvennoe statisticheskoe izdatel'stvo, 1956.

Narodnii Kitai [People's China], 1950–1953.

New China News Agency, *Daily News Release*. Beijing: New China News Agency, 1950.

Nutter, Warren G. *Growth of Industrial Production in the Soviet Union*. Princeton, NJ: Princeton University Press, 1962.

Ong, Shao-er. *Labor Problems in Communist China (to February 1953)*. Studies in Chinese Communism, Series III, no. 5. Research Memorandum no. 42. Lackland Air Force Base, TX: U.S. Air Force Personnel and Training Research Center, 1955.

Orleans, Leo A. *Professional Manpower and Education in Communist China*. Washington, DC: U.S. Government Printing Office, 1961.

People's China. Beijing: Foreign Language Press, 1950-1952.

People's Daily, 1949–1953.

Pepper, Suzanne. "The KMT–CCP Conflict 1945–1949." In *Republican China 1912–1939, Part II*. Vol. 13 of *The Cambridge History of China*. Ed. John K. Fairbank and Albert Feuerwerker, pp. 723–82. Cambridge: Cambridge University Press, 1986.

Pichaluofu, D. "How the Polish Labor Unions Struggle to Improve Industry." *Zhongguo gongye* [Chinese industry] 2 (September 1950): 3.

Pravda, 1946–1949.

Prybyla, Jan S. *The Political Economy of Communist China*. Scranton, PA: International Textbook, 1970.

Qian Gufeng. *Sidalin pailaide ren* [The men whom Stalin sent]. Shanghai: Laodong chubanshe, 1953.

Qingniantuan gongkuang xiaozu gongzuo jingyan [The experience of youth small groups in factories and mines]. Beijing: Qingnian chubanshe, 1951.

Remyga, V. N. *Sistema upravleniya promyshlennost'yu KNR (1949–1975)* [The industrial management system of the PRC, 1949–1975]. Diss. abstract. Moscow: Institute of the Far East, 1977.

Richman, Barry. *Industrial Society in Communist China.* Cambridge: Cambridge University Press, 1977.

Rogachevskaya, L. S. *Sotsialisticheskoe sorevnovanie v SSSR: istoricheskie ocherki* [Socialist competition in the USSR: Historical studies]. Moscow: Nauka, 1977.

Rosenberg, William G., and Marilyn B. Young. *Transforming Russia and China: Revolutionary Struggle in the Twentieth Century.* New York: Oxford University Press, 1982.

Rozenfel'd, Sh. L. *Organizatsiya upravleniya promyshlennost'yu SSSR* [The organization of industrial management in the USSR]. Moscow: Gosplanizdat, 1950.

Rozman, Gilbert. *The Chinese Debate About Soviet Socialism, 1978–1985.* Princeton, NJ: Princeton University Press, 1987.

———. *A Mirror for Socialism: Soviet Criticisms of China.* Princeton, NJ: Princeton University Press, 1985.

Rumyantsev, A. F. *Organizatsiya upravleniya promyshlennost'yu SSSR* [The organization of industrial management in the USSR]. Moscow: Vyshaya partiinaya shkola pri TsK KPSS, 1953.

Sakharov, V. A. *Zarozhdenie i razvitie stakhanovskogo dvizheniya* [The origin and development of the Stakhanovite movement]. Moscow: Izdatel'stvo Moskovsogo universiteta, 1985.

Schapiro, Leonard. *The Communist Party of the Soviet Union.* 2nd ed. New York: Vintage Books, 1971.

Schran, Peter. *Guerrilla Economy: The Development of the Shensi–Kansu–Ninghsia Border Region, 1937–1945.* Albany: State University of New York Press, 1976.

Schurmann, Franz. *Ideology and Organization in Communist China.* 2nd ed. Berkeley and Los Angeles: University of California Press, 1968.

Selden, Mark. *The Yenan Way in Revolutionary China.* Cambridge, MA: Harvard University Press, 1971.

Shandong ribao [Shandong daily], 1950–1951.

Shanxi ribao [Shanxi daily], 1950.

Shchepanskii, V. N. *Massogo-politicheskaya rabota na zavode* [Mass-political work at the factory]. Moscow: Gospolitizdat, 1949.

Shehui zhuyi bisai zai Sulian [Socialist competition in the Soviet Union]. Beiping: Zhongwai chubanshe, 1949.

Shengchan zhongde xuanchuan guli [Propaganda and encouragement in production]. N.p.: 1950?

Shi Liang, ed. *Gongchang guanli gailun* [An introduction to factory management]. Shanghai: Liyanhui tushe yongpinshe chuban, 1952.

Shi Ming Hu and Eli Seifman, eds. *Toward a New World Outlook*. New York: AMS Press, 1976.

Shi Zhe. "I Accompanied Chairman Mao." *Far Eastern Affairs* 2 (1989):125–33.

Siegelbaum, Lewis H. *Stakhanovism and the Politics of Productivity in the USSR, 1935–1941*. Cambridge: Cambridge University Press, 1988.

Skocpol, Theda. *States and Social Revolutions*. Cambridge: Cambridge University Press, 1979.

Sladkovskii, M. I. *Znakomstvo s Kitaem i Kitaitsami* [My acquaintance with China and the Chinese]. Moscow: Mysl', 1984.

Solinger, Dorothy A., ed. *Three Visions of Chinese Socialism*. Boulder, CO: Westview Press, 1984.

Song Zhengquan. "Research on Increasing Labor Productivity." *Zhongguo gongye* [Chinese industry] 2 (May 1950): 19–23.

Spence, Jonathan D. *To Change China: Western Advisors in China, 1620–1960*. New York: Penguin Books, 1980.

————. *The Search for Modern China*. New York: Norton, 1990.

Suliande gongren [Soviet workers]. Shanghai: Laodong chubanshe, 1951.

Tao Fen. *Shiye guanli yu zhiye xiuyang* [Enterprise management and occupational training]. Beijing: Shenghuo, dushu, xinzhi sanlian shudian, 1950.

Teiwes, Frederick C. "Establishment and Consolidation of the New Regime." In *The People's Republic, Part I*. Ed. Roderick MacFarquhar and John K. Fairbank, pp. 51–143. Vol. 14 of *The Cambridge History of China*. Cambridge: Cambridge University Press, 1987.

————. "Mao and His Lieutenants." *Australian Journal of Chinese Affairs* 19–20 (1988): 1–80.

————. *Politics at Mao's Court*. Armonk, NY: M. E. Sharpe, 1990.

Tel'pukhovskii, V. B., ed. *Rabochii klass SSSR v gody uprocheniya i razvitiya sotsialisticheskogo obshchestva 1945–1960 gg.* [The working class of the USSR during the years of consolidation and development of socialist society, 1945–1960]. Vol. 4. Moscow: Nauka, 1987.

Ten Great Years: Statistics of the Economic and Cultural Achievements of the People's Republic of China. Beijing: Foreign Languages Press, 1959.

Tianjin City Labor Union, ed. *Gongye shengchan zhongde zerenzhi jianchazhi lianxi hetong* [The responsibility system, inspection system and related contracts in industrial production]. Tianjin: Zhishi shudian, 1950.

Treadgold, Donald W., ed. *Soviet and Chinese Communism: Similarities and Differences*. Seattle: University of Washington Press, 1967.

Tucker, Robert C. *Stalin in Power: The Revolution from Above, 1928–1941*. New York: Norton, 1990.

————. "Stalinism as Revolution from Above." In *Stalinism: Essays in Historical Interpretation*. Ed. Robert C. Tucker, pp. 106–8. New York: Norton, 1977.

USSR–China in the Changing World. Moscow: Novosti Press Agency Publishing House, 1989.

Vogel, Ezra. *Canton Under Communism: Programs and Politics in a Provincial Capital, 1949–1968*. New York: Harper & Row, 1969.

Volkogonov, Dmitri. *Stalin: Triumph and Tragedy.* Ed. and trans. Harold Shukman. London: Weidenfeld and Nicolson, 1991.

Voronkov, I. I., ed. *Ekonomika i organizatsiya proizvodstva* [Economics and organization of production]. Moscow and Sverdlovsk: Gosudarstvennoe nauchno-tekhnicheskoe izdatel'stvo machinostroitel'noi literatury, 1954.

Vostanovlenie narodnogo khozyaistva SSSR. Sozdanie ekonomiki razvitogo sotsialisma. 1946–nachalo 1960–kh godov [Restoration of the national economy of the USSR. The creation of an economy of developed socialism. 1946–the beginning of the 1960s]. Vol. 6. Moscow: Nauka, 1980.

Walder, Andrew G. *Communist Neo-Traditionalism; Work and Authority in Chinese Industry.* Berkeley and Los Angeles: University of California Press, 1986.

———. "Some Ironies of the Maoist Legacy in Industry." In *The Transition to Socialism in China.* Ed. Mark Selden and Victor Lippit, pp. 215–37. Armonk, NY: M. E. Sharpe, 1982.

Westney, D. Eleanor. *Imitation and Innovation: The Transfer of Western Organizational Patterns to Meiji Japan.* Cambridge: Cambridge University Press, 1987.

Wheatcroft, S. G. "On Assessing the Size of Forced Concentration Camp Labour in the Soviet Union 1929–1956." *Soviet Studies* 33 (April 1981): 267–68.

White, Lynn T., III. *Politics of Chaos: The Organizational Causes of Violence in China's Cultural Revolution.* Princeton, NJ: Princeton University Press, 1989.

Whyte, Martin K. "Bureaucracy and Modernization in China: The Maoist Critique." *American Sociological Review* 38 (April 1973): 149–63.

Williams, Robin M., Jr. *American Society: A Sociological Interpretation.* 3rd ed. New York: Knopf, 1970.

Wilson, Jeanne L. "Trade Unions in Communist States; the People's Republic of China." Wheaton College, 1988. Unpublished manuscript.

Women zenyang guanli qiye [How we manage an enterprise]. Beijing: Gongren chubanshe, 1951.

Wu Qingyou. *Sulian gongye guanli* [*Soviet Enterprise Management*]. Shanghai: Zhonghua shuju yinxing, 1950.

Wu Shushen. "A Discussion on Deliberating the Selection of the Workshop Manager." *Zhongguo gongye* [Chinese industry] 1 (October 1949): 24–25.

Wu Xiuquan. *Zai waijiaobu ba nian de jingli (1950.1–1958.10)* [Eight years in the Foreign Ministry (January 1950–October 1958)]. Beijing: Shijie zhishi chubanshe, 1983.

Xiang gongchan zhuyi quanjinde Sulian qingnian [Soviet youth forge ahead under Communism]. Hankou: Zhongnan qingnian chushe chuban, 1952.

Xianjin shengchan xiaozu [Small groups for advanced production]. Beijing: Gongren chubanshe, 1951.

Xiao Ling and Xiao Yun, eds. *Xin gongren duben* [The new workers' textbook]. Shanghai: Xuesheng shudian faxing, 1949.

Xuanchuan gongzuo wenyi [Collected propaganda works]. Hankou: Zhongnan renmin chubanshe, 1951.

Xuanchuanyuan gongzuo shouce [Handbook of propagandists' work]. Shanghai: Huadong renmin chubanshe, 1951.

Xuanchuanyuan shouce [A manual for propagandists]. Dongbei: Xinhua shudian, 1951.

Yeh, K.C. "Soviet and Communist China Industrialization Strategies." In *Soviet and Chinese Communism: Similarities and Differences.* Ed. Donald W. Treadgold. Seattle: University of Washington Press, 1967.

Zaleski, Eugene. *Stalinist Planning for Economic Growth, 1933–1952.* Chapel Hill: University of North Carolina Press, 1980.

Zenyang gonggu gongchang zhongde xuanchuanwang [How to strengthen the factory propaganda network]. Shanghai: Huadong renmin chubanshe, 1951.

Zhao Dexin, ed. *Gongren jieji he gongchandang* [The working class and the Communist party]. Beijing: Gongren chubanshe, 1952.

Zheng Hongshu. "How Soviet Enterprise Management Is Regulated, pt. 1." *Zhongguo gongye* [Chinese industry] 2 (June 1950): 21–25.

———. "How Soviet Enterprise Management Is Regulated, pt. 2." *Zhongguo gongye* [Chinese industry] 2 (July 1950): 7–14.

———. "The Relationship Between Soviet Labor Unions and Economic Development." *Zhongguo gongye* [Chinese industry] 1 (December 1949): 27–32.

———. "Socialist Competition and the Stakhanov Movement." *Zhongguo gongye* [Chinese industry] 1 (January 1950): 27–36.

Zhongguo gongye [Chinese industry]. Shanghai: Zhongguo gongye yuekanshe, 1949–1953.

Zhongguo zong shumu [Chinese general title catalogue]. Beijing: Xinhua shudian biandian, 1955.

Zhou Ming. "Notes from a Visit to a Moscow Knitting Factory." *Gongren ribao*, December 2, 1949, p. 5.

Zhu Cishou., ed. *Gongchan laodong jingji* [The economics of factory labor]. Shanghai: Lixin huiji tushu yongpinshe chuban, 1951.

Zhu Cishou. "How Does the Soviet Union Increase Labor Productivity in Industry?" *Zhongguo gongye* [Chinese industry] 2 (May 1950): 3–9.

Zhu Pu. "The Great New Records Movement." *Zhongguo gongye* [Chinese industry] 1 (December 1950): 3–16.

Zhuravlev, A. *Agitator–organizator sotsialisticheskogo sorevnovaniya* [The agitator is the organizer of socialist competition]. Moscow: Gospolitizdat, 1948.

Zukin, Sharon, and Paul DiMaggio, eds. *Structures of Capital.* Cambridge: Cambridge University Press, 1990.

Index